THE LITTLE HOUSE
at
SANDY NECK

Edward Otis Handy, Jr.

Cover watercolor by Robert Mesrop

For my tolerant wife and family
and for all who cherish Barnstable.

Published by Edward Otis Handy, Jr.

West Barnstable Press
ISBN 0-9816873-6-9

Library of Congress Control Number: 2008938241

To purchase a copy of this book, contact:
Edward Otis Handy, Jr.
P.O. Box 403, Barnstable, Massachusetts 02630
508-362-3444

TABLE OF CONTENTS

PREFACE

This book is about Cape Cod. More particularly, it's about Barnstable Harbor, Sandy Neck, the vast marsh it embraces, and an isolated gunning camp that has stood in the marsh for almost 100 years.

It includes some local history and lore and, here and there, a cherished memory of a notable person, story or recipe garnered during a long life lived on a changing Cape Cod in a changing world. For over 30 years a log has been kept at the camp. It is quoted liberally with syntax and grammar "as is", undisturbed by well-intentioned editing.

The book pretends nothing serious or profound. It is to be taken with a glass of wine and recognized as an invitation to share pleasures derived from a remote shelter in a place of rare interest and beauty.

One of my adult children asked why it was written. I have never heard a swan's song and, being 79 and slightly deaf, probably never will. But it is easy to imagine what a swan might sing about: its loves and joys and the sweet-sorrow of life on this planet. Finding the theme compelling, but being neither swan nor singer, I chose pen and paper to express my abiding love for the harbor, marsh and dunes and my concerns for their future.

Come along! Walk the dunes, dig a clam or two, meet Braley Jenkins, watch a sunset, hear children's voices, taste Janet's mussels and, above all, enjoy some of the history and magic of Sandy Neck, Barnstable Harbor and the Great Marsh.

PART ONE

Barnstable Harbor, the Great Marsh and Sandy Neck

"A noble prospect is seen from the high grounds . . . A very extensive salt marsh, at that time covered with several thousand stacks of hay; the harbor, a mile wide, and four or five miles long; a long, lofty, wild and fantastical beach thrown into a 1000 grotesque forms by the united force of wind and waves." Timothy Dwight, president of Yale, describing the Great Marsh, Barnstable Harbor and Sandy Neck (1810).

Mr. Dwight was looking east. This is near the east end looking west.

Chapter One

PATHWAY TO THE SEA

Since Indians paddled their canoes out to the oyster beds and Bartholomew Gosnold visited in 1602 (as some historians believe he did), maritime use of Barnstable Harbor has undergone a sea change. We do know that a Pilgrim shallop with ten men sailed from Plymouth into Barnstable Harbor in August of 1621 to find the lost and troublesome boy, John Billington. Late that year Governor Winslow wrote about the hard sail they had:

"...ere we had been long at sea, there arose a storm of wind and rain, with much lightning and thunder, insomuch that a spout arose not far from us. But, GOD be praised! it dured not long: and we put in, that night, for harbor, at a place, called Cummaquid; where we had some hope to find the boy...It being night, before we came in; we anchored in the midst of the bay; where we were dry [aground] at low water.

In the morning, we espied savages seeking lobsters..." Billington was ultimately saved through the good offices of " . . . their Sachem or Governor, who they call IYANOUGH, a man not exceeding twenty-six years of age; but very personable [comely], gentle, courteous, and fair conditioned: indeed not like a savage except for his attire . . . his cheer plentiful and various."

Nestled against the Harbor and the Great Marsh are the villages of Barnstable and West Barnstable. From both hailed outstanding sailors who as boys must have viewed the Harbor as an exciting pathway to adventure, fame and fortune. From Barnstable village came William Sturgis and Daniel Bacon, both leaders in the China trade. Sturgis made five trips to China, commanding his first ship at 19. He retired from the sea in 1810 at age 28 and became a leading Boston merchant controlling much of the maritime business in the Pacific. Daniel Bacon, first mate on the last trip of Captain Sturgis, helped repulse an attack by 16 pirate vessels. Subsequently he commanded four more China voyages and later became a major Boston ship owner, said to be one of the first to appreciate the potential of the clipper ship. Captain John Percival, known as

"Mad Jack", was born in West Barnstable and is best known for having commanded the *Constitution* in the years 1844-1846 throughout its 52,279 mile voyage around the world.

Many Barnstable families have their favorite sea stories to spin. One neighbor tells about two vessels passing in the Harbor mouth. The packet announced it was from Yarmouth and asked the ship where it hailed from. The answer floated back "China". Here are three of my family stories to remind one how proximate the sea has always been to life on Cape Cod.

James Delap reached Barnstable in 1729 under unusual circumstances. These are the facts as told by his great-grandson Amos Otis in his *Genealogical Notes of Barnstable Families*. One Charles Clinton, a man of wealth and influence, persuaded over 100 of his friends to emigrate with him from Ireland to America. Included were James Delap, then 14, his father, mother and three sisters. Clinton chartered the ship *George and Ann* and hired a Captain Rymer to transport the emigrants and their effects from Dublin to Philadelphia. "Mr. Clinton was unfortunate in his selection of a ship; but more unfortunate in his selection of a captain. Rymer was a cold blooded tyrant, of whom his officers and sailors were in constant fear, and as base a villain as ever trod the deck of a slave ship." It developed that Rymer was intent upon starving all the passengers and making off with their possessions. The ship was eventually boarded off Chatham by one Captain Lothrop of Barnstable. By this time many of the passengers had perished including all of the Delaps except James and his mother. She "...was living when Captain Lothrop came on board-emaciated and very weak, in consequence of [starvation]... When food was distributed she took a biscuit, and in attempting to swallow it a piece lodged in her throat, and before relief could be obtained, expired... James, when taken from the boat, was so weak that he could not stand, and crawled from the boat to the beach." Rymer sailed the ship on to Philadelphia where his "... sailors relieved from the terror in which they had been held, entered a complaint against their Captain. He was arrested, a preliminary examination was had, and he was sent in irons to England for trial. The charges of cruelty to his passengers and crew, of extortion, and of an attempt to embezzle the goods of the passengers were proved, and he was condemned to be hung and quartered, and this just sentence was duly executed in Dublin."

2

Mr. Otis goes on to tell about his grandfather, Amos Otis, and his brother-in-law, Thomas Delap (son of James Delap), who "...was master of a vessel, in the King's service, Dec. 6, 1771, while on a voyage from Philadelphia to Halifax, during a violent gale and snow storm was cast ashore on Great Point, Nantucket. All on board succeeded in getting to the shore. It was a thick snow storm and very cold. Mr. Delap perished in one of the hollows or gorges on that point, Mr. Amos Otis in another. Two of the sailors went on to Cortue Point, heading towards the town, and both froze to death on that point. Two other sailors and a boy, John Weiderhold, succeeded in getting off Great Point, and reached a barn at Squam. They covered themselves up in hay, placing the lad between them, so that the warmth of their bodies kept him from freezing.

The next day the vessel was discovered by people from the town, high and dry on the beach, and if the captain and crew had remained on board none would have been lost. Capt. Delap, Mr. Otis, and most of the crew, had been exposed to the storm about twelve hours when the vessel was cast on shore, and were wet, benumbed with cold, and almost exhausted, when they got to land. The boy was the only one who had not been exposed, and who had dry clothing. ...The boy, Weiderhold, from that time made Nantucket his home....He often related the sad story of the shipwreck, and pointed out the spots where each perished."

Thomas Delap and his brother-in-law, Amos Otis, are buried in Nantucket. The grave stone of Mr. Otis bears the following inscription: "Here lies Amos Otis of Barnstable, son of Solomon Otis, Esq. And Jane, his wife. He was cast ashore on Nantucket December ye 6th, 1771, and perished in ye snow storm there aged thirty-four years."

John Otis, grandson of the Amos who died in Nantucket and my great-great-grandfather, left Barnstable and a pregnant bride in the 1820s to sail as captain of a ship that was lost at sea. The ship never returned and Captain Otis, according to family records, was killed in a mutiny.

Look now to the harbor which Timothy Dwight saw from his hill in 1810. It plays a key role in this book.

Protected on the north by the spectacular, glowing white dunes of Sandy Neck, some over 60 feet high, changed hourly by its sweeping tides, Barnstable Harbor has to be one of the most beautiful on the East Coast. The marsh (fringing the south of the Neck) transforms from brilliant velvety greens to burnished gold as the seasons change. Tides vary from nine and a half to eleven or more feet changing twice daily, each flushing in and out some 93,000,000 cubic feet of water. There is ten times as much water at high tide as at low when 60% of the Harbor bottom is uncovered, exposing extensive mud and sand flats, leaving at the west end nothing more than ribbon channels, shallow and narrow. Towards the entrance at the east the channels deepen and are navigable at low tide. Elsewhere low water and no water are much the same.

Summer water temperatures range from the mid-sixties to the seventies, considerably warmer than Cape Cod Bay. When the incoming tide flows over warming flats and covers the marshes with shallow pools that cook in the sun, the ebb tide can be unusually warm, even reaching the low eighties. The water is clear and the bottom primarily sandy and free from growth.

A distant view of the cottage colony and east end of Sandy Neck.

At its east end the Harbor opens into Cape Cod Bay. The major channel moving east from the Barnstable shore swings north to Sandy Neck and flows along the cottage colony on the Point next to the old once-abandoned lighthouse. The "back flats" behind the Neck on the Bay side are now crowded at low tides in the summer time: our relatively new population of small and bigger motor boats tend to flock there and leave the upper Harbor for clams, shorebirds and smaller craft.

Across the channel from the Point are the Yarmouth flats, miles of rippled sand with pools for children to explore and drop offs where fly fishermen ply their sport in hot pursuit of striped bass and the odd bluefish. Not only are these environs a varied and picturesque playground, for years they have provided food and livelihood for a hardy race of watermen, those who harvest fish, shellfish and wildfowl here in weather pleasant and otherwise.

Hunters and gatherers cherish low tide while high water is the sailor's delight.

Chapter Two

THE HAYING FIELDS

By 1639 Barnstable had acquired enough population to incorporate. Town records for 1643/1644 list 45 men as inhabitants including Thomas Hinckley, governor of the Plymouth colony, more Hinckleys, Henry Cobb, Nathaniel Bacon and others. These early residents came to be known as the "First Comers". In 1697 the Great Marsh was divided among the First Comers and their descendants who in the same year were organized into a body politic known as the "Proprietors" with responsibility for dividing up the common lands.

The Great Marsh looking east from West Barnstable by Charles D. Cahoon.

The Great Marsh, sometimes called the "haying fields", is the 4.8 square miles of high marsh protected by Sandy Neck. These flat salt meadows at approximately mean high tide level produced the plentiful salt hay that helped to bring the First Comers to Barnstable. Salt hay was used to feed and bed down livestock, to insulate houses, and much later as a packing material for the bricks made in West Barnstable. It was harvested in late August on the low tides with the help of horses and wagons, the horses footed with round, wooden bog shoes. Timothy Dwight as late as 1810 commented on several thousand piles of hay drying in the Barnstable marsh. The fresh cut hay was stacked on staddles to dry and to permit the maximum harvest on a given day. A "staddle" was a circle of poles sunk into the marsh that could hold a couple of tons of hay above the flood tide. Reportedly there were as many as 1000 staddles still in the Great Marsh in 1898 when most of them were taken out by the Portland Storm, a major disaster that sank the *City of Portland* off Provincetown.

The *City of Portland* courtesy of the Maine Historical Society.

At seven o'clock on Saturday evening, November 26, 1898, the *City of Portland*, a palatial side wheeler 261 feet long and 62 feet wide, left India Wharf in Boston bound for Portland, Maine. The weather was threatening but in Captain Blanchard's opinion manageable. In the course of the night and the next day conditions grew worse, the vessel was disabled and ultimately sank off Provincetown. The passengers and crew, believed to number 191, were all lost along with the passenger manifest. Time pieces found on recovered bodies had stopped at 9:15 but whether the ship sank in the morning or evening of the 27th is not known. *The Barnstable Patriot* of November 28, 1898, reports "The most severe storm in years set in about 9 o'clock Saturday evening and by midnight was a howling gale. All day Sunday the gale continued accompanied with sleet and rain. The wind blew at a velocity of sixty to seventy miles an hour and trees, chimneys, windmills and fences were laid low all about town . . . It being on the full of the moon the tides are running high, it being full sea at about 11 o'clock, and the gale backed the sea up into the bay and the railroad track was covered in places. At the brick-yard at West Barnstable about 300 feet of the track was washed out."

The next issue of the *Patriot* which came out on December 5th described losses of many ships and lives, some daring rescues and a 150 to 200 ton wrecked vessel beached on the back of Sandy Neck. Also a Mr. Liscomb, agent of the owners of the *City of Portland*, is quoted in the same edition:

"Captain Blanchard took a fearful responsibility. I personally ordered him not to leave before 9 o'clock, and not to go then if the storm was thick. …He assumed a fearful responsibility."

The paper describes the violence of the storm in Sandwich. "The severest moment was at about 10 A.M. when the gale seemed to take an exceptional spurt and leveled everything in its path. From fifteen to twenty of our fine, large elms on Main Street were uproot-ed and thrown across the road, chimneys on many houses fell with terrific crashes….The roof of the Cape Cod Glass Factory was destroyed…The railroad from this point was twisted and thrown out of shape …Such a storm and gale was never known in this vicin-ity, and much of the damage can never be replaced…" The water was so high that it flooded the cellars of houses along Main Street in Barnstable village.

Not surprising that most of the 1000 remaining staddles were wiped out by the Portland Storm.

While the harvesting of salt hay diminished in importance, in the early decades of the 1900s it continued to be used for bedding ani-mals and as mulch. Since it spoiled the taste of milk, it was not a favored food for cows. William F. Bodfish, a life-long West Barnstable resident, was born in 1877 and died in 1970 at age 93. The last to cut hay in the Great Marsh, he drove his horse-drawn hay wagon until two years before his death when his 34 year old horse died. He recalled herding cattle from the Cape to a slaughter house in Brighton, floating houses from Nantucket on barges and hauling them from Barnstable Harbor with teams of oxen and taking hunters to camps on Sandy Neck by horse-drawn wagon.

No longer renowned as haying fields, the Great Marsh continues to be of interest for duck hunting, clamming and as an extraor-dinarily prolific source of food for surrounding sea and bird life.

Chapter Three

THE FANTASTICAL BEACH

In 1810 Timothy Dwight described Sandy Neck as *"...a long, lofty, wild and fantastical beach thrown into a 1000 grotesque forms by the united force of wind and waves..."* A satellite photograph of Cape Cod shows predominantly smooth shorelines highlighted with a filigree of bright-sand beaches. Along-shore currents tend to eat away projections and to deposit barrier beaches across coastal indentations. The barrier beach called Sandy Neck began about 4000 years ago to reach eastward from Sandwich toward Dennis and as it grew its strong arm embraced and shielded the Great Marsh and Barnstable Harbor against the ravages of the prevailing winter north wind. Today it extends some six miles easterly toward the Dennis shore falling short because of the immense twice-daily flow of water in and out of the Harbor around the end of the Neck, known as Beach Point or, locally, the Point. Someday perhaps Sandy Neck will reach Dennis and the Harbor will become an enclosed salt pond like those on the south shore of Martha's Vineyard, but many moons will pass before that happens. Meanwhile the Neck acts as a protective barrier for a total of 8.3 square miles including 4.8 square miles of high marsh and 3.5 square miles of harbor and developing marsh.

The Neck is a long, wild, unoccupied and undeveloped peninsula of wind-sculpted sand dunes with barren beach on Cape Cod Bay to the north and marsh and Harbor on the south. Other than by foot or horse, travel is by four-wheel-drive vehicle only and then is strictly limited. In its low areas are impenetrable patches of bayberries, cat briers, beach plums and other shrubs surrounding and interweaving the bogs of cranberries. At various points there are extensive stands of pine and scrub oak with occasional junipers and holly trees. Some of the woods are open, free of undergrowth with wind-pruned pitch pines that grow only to the dune tops and compensate at sand level by branching out to create a striking ground cover. Children think the dunes their own limitless sand box and tumbling down them has brought squeals of delight for generations. From a dune top on a bright summer day, looking north one sees the deep blue of Cape Cod Bay, at the southwest are the velvet green marshes laced with silver creeks and to the southeast the Harbor and its activities. The mainland of the Cape is the back drop on the south, high glacial moraine now covered with second and third growth and houses, mostly built after the 1940s and the end of World War II. A mile south from the dunes, the signs of civilization are seen in miniature like a toy village.

Indians were the first users, testified to by the many shell heaps, or middens, still found in the dune declivities. There was a tribal village on Scorton Hill at the base of the Neck. Come summer, so the story goes, the residents migrated to the Neck to be closer to the plentiful shellfish. Shells of oysters, hard and soft shell clams, mussels and scallops abound in the middens. Most now have probably been well picked over for implements, pipes, arrowheads, pottery shards and other signs of good Indian living. Professor George Lyman Kittredge, a long time Barnstable resident, in the course of his visits to the dunes amassed an outstanding collection of artifacts, many of which are at the local historical society. Arrow heads are still found sometimes and chips of quartz where they were made. Think of the long summer nights in the dunes, with great fires and round-the-clock clam bakes - not a bad way of life. Since clams were readily available, the Indians may well have spent much of the year in the dunes varying their diet with venison, meat from drift whales and blackfish, now and then a duck or goose with oysters, blueberries and cranberries, each in their season.

This romantic view of Indian life does tend to gainsay the hazards of real romance. Taisto Ranta, the Sandy Neck ranger, was doing his rounds on Sandy Neck following a windy stretch of weather when he discovered a newly exposed Indian shell heap. A bone protruded that turned out to be next to a human skull. After the police were notified the state anthropologist came to the site and a careful excavation was done. After further examination in Boston, it was determined that the bones were of a female and dated back some 500 years. The skeleton was complete and in perfect condition including the teeth which showed no cavities. The skull, however, was damaged over one eye. According to Taisto, the anthropologist thought perhaps she had said no to the wrong chief. To deviate a bit, there is more to Taisto's story. After the technical examination was completed, neither Town nor State officials knew what to do with the skeleton, so they put it in a box and returned it to Taisto pending further instructions. About seven years slipped by while Taisto guarded the box and finally, pursuant to long-delayed official instructions, the box and contents were turned over to the local Wampanoag tribe for reburial.

When the First Comers reached Barnstable they commandeered the Neck for their own purposes. In the late 1600s and early 1700s the north shore, the so-called "back beach", was intensively used for inshore whaling. Right whales were the favored prey because they swam close to the beach and, more important, they floated when killed. Whale boats were stationed along the shore where they could be quickly launched and rowed out when a passing whale was spotted. If all worked according to plan the harpooner would make fast to the whale which would drag the boat until exhausted and then be killed and rowed ashore. The flensing or removal of strips of blubber was accomplished on the back beach. Then the blubber was hauled toward the Harbor side into a "try yard" for "trying" or boiling out the oil. When the Neck was divided in 1715 into 60 lots and turned over to the Proprietors, four try yards on the south were reserved for common use along with rights of way from the back beach. A strip of land along the back beach was also reserved for common use where shelters could be built for the whalers who watched and waited. The authority on this subject is a book by John Braginton Smith and Duncan Oliver titled *Cape Cod Shore Whaling America's First Whalemen* and for more detail is quoted here. "One of the shore whalefishermen's western locations on Cape Cod Bay was Sandy Neck in Barnstable. The Rev. John Mellen, writing in 1794, noted: 'Seventy or eighty years ago the whale bay fishery was carried on in boats from shore, to great advantage. This business employed nearly two hundred men for three months of the year, the fall, and the beginning of winter. But few whales now come into the bay, and this kind of fishery has for a long time (by this town at least) been given up...' The Proprietors took special care with land on Sandy Neck, reserving pathways and convenient access to try yards and houses. Housing for the whalefishermen was on the north side of the neck...where observers could watch for whales...Their try yards were on the marsh side...Horses pulled carts containing pieces of blubber cut from the whale across the sand from the back beach to the south side dunes... where the try pots were located...These whale houses were large, permanent structures with cellars in which New England rum doubtless was stored against the cold and long evenings. They contained bunks to sleep in, and in the evening, over their flip, these men told their whaling stories". In the course of trying the whales much of the wood on private property was casually expropriated and in time regulations were adopted to control the problem.

Right whales to harvest, and with them inshore whaling, passed off the Sandy Neck scene in the early 1700s.

An endangered northern right whale. Adults typically weigh over 100 tons and are 35 to 55 feet long. Today only 300 to 400 are believed to exist.

Chapter Four

TRY YARD MEADOW

Having divided the Great Marsh among the First Comers in 1697, in 1715 the Proprietors laid out Sandy Neck in 60 lots "as equal in value as may bee for Quantity & Quality Considered spesiall Regard being hasd to ye wood Reserving Priviledg & use of four spots or pesses for the setting up four Try houses of about half an acre to each for ye Laying blubber barrils wood & other nessessaries for ye trying of oyl as need may Require Reserving or leaving all Convenient waies pticulerly waies from ye 20 rods Reserved on ye north shoare to sd try houses & so down ye south shoare for Landing bots & tacking of oyl & what else may be necessary…" Wood on the Neck was growing increasingly scarce and a price was ordained by earlier regulation. The trying of blubber required great fires and consumed much wood. The 60 parcels were divided amongst residents who made their choice by lot. This was all done at the tail end of the on-shore whaling era but careful provision was made for the industry that must have garnered considerable wealth. The 60 lots comprising Sandy Neck bordered south on the marsh which had previously been parceled out so the try yards reserved in 1715 were in the interior of the Neck where the wood was in best supply and the blubber was closest to its source.

One of the try yards was located about half way out to the Point where the Neck was wide and wood relatively plentiful; thus the actual boiling down of the blubber was done in the dunes and the barreled oil brought across the marsh for shipping. Conveniently the marsh was narrow at this point with good access to the Harbor for transportation to the mainland. And this piece of marsh that had been parceled out to a First Comer in 1697 came to be known as Try Yard Meadow.

The story of the ownership of Try Yard Meadow reveals some important and some quaint local history and attitudes. Try Yard Meadow was first referred to in the will of Benjamin Gorham, Jr. who died in 1798. It refers to property inherited from John Russell "…now improved by Daniel Davis, Esq. in the right of his wife

Mehitable." She was an unusual woman of that era, one who survived five children, lived to 87 and outlasted four husbands. Her property went to her daughter, Sarah Parker, whose 5/12ths interest in Try Yard Meadow was combined with Abigail Bacon's 7/12ths interest and in 1826 conveyed to Josiah Hinckley (1794-1883).

On October 22, 1827, Josiah and a friend were playing cards in Sally Crocker's Tavern, across the street from the County House the night it burned. The two got a ladder, went to the fire and managed to save some probate papers and one volume of deeds. Ninety-three real estate folios, three volumes of probate records and civil and criminal court papers were lost leaving a gap of over 100 years for historians to bridge. Title records from 1697 to 1827 were lost. In later years. Josiah remembered climbing to the second floor of the building where the fire looked him "...full in the face and seemed to say...you had better stand back and make room for me." We know he did stand back; that he was Barnstable born and bred; that he owned and operated a thriving lumber business at the end of Rendezvous Lane almost directly across the Harbor from Try Yard Meadow; that he was president of the local savings bank; that he had six children; and that in all respects he was a man of accomplishment. In 1878 he deeded Try Yard Meadow to his eldest son, Lothrop Hinckley.

Josiah's 1883 obituary from the *Patriot* notes with considerable relish that he was a direct descendent of Governor Thomas Hinckley, Rev. John Lothrop, Rev. John Robinson and various members of the Davis and Gorham families, good Barnstable folk. Josiah, it observes "...came of excellent New England stock and it would be a noticeable deviation from ancestral types had he not possessed and illustrated throughout a long life well-balanced characteristics of both lines of descent. It is not necessary to enter into the subject of transmission and effect of commingling of individual traits by marriage in the above lines of descent where a life of nearly ninety years spent in this village of his birth which he loved so ardently, is rounded off with the strict integrity of character, an example so clean of vulgarity and profanity in his domestic life and in the daily pursuits of his avocations and public relations 'His heart as far from fraud as Heaven from Earth.' Not alone does his death create a void in the every day scenes in our streets and by-ways, where from youth to old age his presence has been familiar to three generations, but a greater void in the home of his and his children's birth now first broken at its foundation, his wife, Mercy Crocker, having preceded him only a few weeks at the advanced age of nearly eighty-seven years, having in their sixty-eight years of married and domestic life redeemed their plight of troths at the alter, discharged every obligation that parental and domestic life imposed, leaving to their children fond and enduring recollections to heal the wound that bereavement feels. Mr. Hinckley was for many years Town Clerk, Collector and Treasurer, represented the town in the General Court several terms; ...was appointed Justice of the Peace...; was commissioned Collector of the Customs by President Polk...; was elected County Treasurer five successive years...discharging his duties in the several offices with conscientious integrity. Well posted in colonial and local history, and having a keen recollection and love of everything of local interest and associated with the past which he had heard related by his mother who died in 1856 aged 87... And his Lothrop grandmother who died in 1828, aged 80 years, rendered him a connecting link with the early period of 1750 and a store-house of traditions, facts, anecdotes and incidents in connection with persons and places in the town...."

Ten years after his father deeded Try Yard Meadow to him, Lothrop Hinckley was run over by a train. The records about Lothrop are scant, reporting only that he died without a will and that all of his property, including Try Yard Meadow, passed by intestacy to his only surviving child, Mary G. Hinckley. She lived in the family house, never married and served for three three-year terms as assistant register of probate.

In 1911 Mary sold Try Yard Meadow to Walter P. Henderson and the Little House was built thereon as a gunning camp after 1911 but before the 1914 Geodetic Survey map on which it is shown. Title records report several owners in the ensuing years, all duck shooting friends.

During the years of the Second World War, and perhaps for some years before, the property was seldom used, if at all. After the war Gordon Marshall, a well-to-do Bostonian, and Lee Austin, a retired president of Jones & Laughlin Steel Company, moved to Barnstable and built on land across the Harbor from the Little House. Both were ardent duck hunters and took enough interest in the remote gunning camp to track down the owners. A deal was struck with one George Gilbert Smith, the single surviving owner, who was located

Try Yard Meadow and the Little House.

in a nursing home and agreed to sell reserving to himself "...for life the personal right to use said premises on a par ..." with the grantees. Messrs. Austin and Marshall took title in 1945, moved a year-round squatter out and cleaned out years of debris. Among the findings were a set of formal tails said to have belonged to a Russian counsel who came duck shooting after partying and ultimately, like the blind mice, left his tails behind him.

Lee was a near contemporary of my parents and 30 years or more my senior. Although we did some fishing and hunting together, we never shot near, or until later even talked about, the Little House. It's doubtful that they used it much, but Lee and Gordon are long gone and any stories they might have told about their gunning shack are victims now of final censorship. In trying to reconstruct even the recent past, it's surprising and disheartening to discover how much is irretrievably gone.

Chapter Five

PRINCIPAL PLAYERS

These scanty biographical details of some of the people who frequent these pages are here to sharpen your focus and pique your interest.

Charles Lee Austin, Jr. (1902-1992), always known to his friends as Lee, graduated from Princeton in 1924 and was captain of its crew. As a young banker in the 1920s he crossed Russia on the Trans-Siberian Railroad. He married his witty and handsome wife, Louise, in 1928 and went on to become an outstanding business man, ultimately a tycoon in the steel business and consultant for the World Bank. He and Gordon Marshall bought the Little House in 1945 to preserve it, and for duck shooting.

Braley Jenkins Jr. (1812-1894) was a West Barnstable fruit grower who recognized the commercial possibilities of cranberries. He acquired by purchase or possession most of Sandy Neck which was sold after his death for a pittance.

The Kittredges:
George Lyman Kittredge (1860-1941), Harvard's great Shakespeare scholar, grew up in Barnstable. His multitudinous and insatiable interests included the Sandy Neck Indians. Arrow heads and artifacts from his digs can be seen at the local historical society.

His son, **Henry Crocker Kittredge** (1890-1967) called himself "pure juice of the Cape Cod grape". One of the great Cape Cod writers he wrote *Cape Cod; Its People and their History* (1930), *Shipmasters of Cape Cod* (1935) and *Mooncussers of Cape Cod* (1937). He grew up shooting ducks with Alfred Redfield and Marcus Howes, had a rustic gunning camp deep in the marshes on the Neck and his own little house near the point which he called the Barnacle.

Alfred Clarence Redfield (1890-1983) summered as a boy in Barnstable, graduated and got his doctorate from Harvard, became a professor there and chaired its biology department, then moved back to the Cape and became associate director of Woods Hole Oceanographic Institution. He was an early officer of the Barnstable Yacht Club, a duck hunter, and wrote extensively on matters concerning the New England coastline. Many of the facts about the Harbor and the Neck cited here are derived from his articles entitled *Ontogeny of a Salt Marsh Estuary* from January 1, 1965 *Science*, Vol. 165, and *Development of a New England Salt Marsh*, a contribution to and accepted by Woods Hole Oceanographic Institution in 1971. His experiments with Marcus Howes on clam propagation in the Harbor were productive.

Marcus Howes (1881-1959) was a classic waterman, who lived his life working the Harbor until he died in Barnstable. He was a duck guide and market gunner, a clam digger and clam propagator and when he died there was little to be found about him in the records. But everyone of an age in Barnstable remembers Marc Howes and some recall that he did enjoy a good drink.

Taisto Ranta (1920-) grew up on his family's West Barnstable farm helping to take care of 1500-2000 laying chickens, three hogs, two work horses and three cows. The family supplied the Cape Cod Hospital with eggs and milk from 1924 until World War II. For the Town of Barnstable he was winter game warden from 1962 until he retired in 1982, the Sandy Neck police officer from 1963 until his retirement and for many years he served in the Natural Resources Department, finally as its Director. At this time in life he tends his fine garden, his productive bees and maintains an enviable twinkle. His extensive experiences and knowledge of the Harbor and Sandy Neck make his contributions to this book invaluable.

Tim Coggeshall (1922-   ) is Barnstable's most recent blue-water sailor. He graduated from Harvard in 1943 with a commission in the Navy, served for four years, first on a destroyer escort then a light cruiser, and spent the rest of his working years teaching high school. But come summer time, his love of sailing took the helm and from 1958 for the next 40 years he cruised mostly up and down the Maine coast with a helper and changing crews of children. The usual summer had eight trips with six children on each. Tim has helped with many of the facts and stories about Barnstable sailing.

The Lovells of four generations were quintessential watermen. **Benjamin** and his son **Herbert** (1856-1934) fished, shot and, until the early 1900s, ran the Barnstable Harbor House, an eatery at the Point. Herbert's son **Shirley** (1885-1968) carried on the family tradition operating a fish trap at Mussel Point and selling lobsters caught in his extensive line of pots outside the Harbor. Shirley's son, **Herbert** (1919-1995), carried on his father's operations. Shirley would be enormously proud of his grandsons. One graduated from Yale and put himself through medical school harvesting mussels and working on one of Barnstable's commercial fishing boats; the other operates a sizeable marine business in the Harbor.

The Handys include the author, his wife, Sue; our children Susie, Jeb, Ned (or Bear) and Seth; and grandchildren too numerous to list.

PART TWO

The Early Years

"I must go down to the seas again, to the lonely sea and the sky,
And all I ask is a tall ship and a star to steer her by."

John Masefield, *Sea Fever* (1810).

Cat boats in Barnstable Harbor circa 1900.

Chapter Six

SAIL HO!

In the early days it was much easier to cart goods to and from Boston by boat than by horse or ox and wagon. In the 1660s one Thomas Huckins, a tavern keeper, shipmaster and receiver of excise, charged himself for bringing into Barnstable on his own vessel 179 gallons of spirits, 43 for his own tavern. Huckins seems to have been a well-rounded person with interests in sailing, the tax base and keeping his neighbors in good spirits.

During the early years of the war of 1812 the British harassed local ports in Cape Cod Bay. One Captain Richard Raggett of *H. B. M.'s Spencer* exacted ransoms of $4,000 and $1,200 from Brewster and Eastham, respectively, in his words: "a contribution for the preservation of your Salt Works, which, as I consider of great public utility, will be otherwise destroyed." Meanwhile Barnstable had obtained four cast-iron cannons, perhaps brought from Boston by ox team by Loring Crocker, to protect his salt works. The cannons, two of which today grace the Court House lawn, were situated one pair on the Common Field and the other at Salten Point. They constituted Barnstable's coastal artillery and, perhaps, with a bit of help from the sand bars in Barnstable Harbor, saved Mr. Crocker and his salt works from the heavy $6,000 ransom demanded by Captain Raggett.

Beginning in the 1820s packets, small, swift sloops and schooners ran on regular schedules from Barnstable to Boston. The cost was a dollar or dollar and a half each way and given favorable conditions a one way passage could be finished in seven hours. Or it could take three times as long if wind and seas were uncooperative. Even though the bunks left much to be desired and bilge smells could be overwhelming, travel by packet was favored by most, perhaps because of conviviality and the good New England rum served in the early years. The packets departed from several wharfs in the Harbor and at one time there were five packet masters operating out of Barnstable. As time passed the original fishing schooners tended to be replaced with sleek and fast sloops. With packets sailing out of most of the north side ports, competition was inevitable.

In 1828 the Yarmouth line acquired the *Commodore Hull* designed for speed and to shame the Barnstable ships. And show them her stern and taffrail she did time and time again. Meanwhile a consortium from Barnstable, Daniel Bacon, Matthias Hinckley and Thomas Percival, tired of the humiliation, had the sloop *Mail* built to order in New York, specifically to race and leave the *Commodore Hull* in its wake. Henry Kittredge in *Cape Cod Its People and Their History* best describes their initial race.

"On their first rival voyage for Boston, the two vessels crossed Barnstable Bar abreast, leaving behind them two villages wild with excitement, and many wagers between the inhabitants of each. The watchers from the shore could see no change in their relative positions; neck and neck they tore along before a fresh southerly breeze until they were hull down and lost to sight. The new Barnstable vessel, however, fulfilled her destiny and nosed out the *Commodore Hull*, sliding into Central Wharf a bare three lengths ahead of her rival." So it was a victory for the *Mail*, and the six hour running time was significantly better than usual.

The local newspaper, the *Patriot*, seems to have sponsored the catboat regatta that was held on Friday, August 18, 1882, with a delayed rerun for the "second class" on the following Tuesday. Here's how the issue of August 22, 1882, describes the first day: "What promised to be one of the most exciting events of the season in this section turned out to be a rather tame affair on account of lack of wind. The boats assembled in the vicinity of Scudder's Wharf promptly at the appointed hour and the start was made without a hitch or mishap. It was one of the handsomest sights ever witnessed in this harbor.

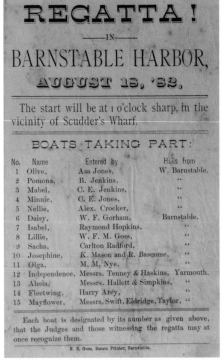

REGATTA !

—IN—

BARNSTABLE HARBOR,

AUGUST 15, '82,

The start will be at 1 o'clock sharp, in the vicinity of Scudder's Wharf.

BOATS TAKING PART:

No.	Name	Entered by	Hails from
1	Olive,	Asa Jones,	W. Barnstable.
2	Pomona,	B. Jenkins,	"
3	Mabel,	C. E. Jenkins,	"
4	Minnie,	C. E. Jones,	"
5	Nellie,	Alex. Crocker,	"
6	Daisy,	W. F. Gorham,	Barnstable.
7	Isabel,	Raymond Hopkins,	"
8	Lillie,	W. F. M. Goss,	"
9	Sacha,	Carlton Radford,	"
10	Josephine,	K. Mason and R. Bascome,	"
11	Olga,	M. M. Nye,	"
12	Independence,	Messrs. Tenney & Haskins,	Yarmouth.
13	Ahola,	Messrs. Hallett & Simpkins,	"
14	Fleetwing,	Harry Arey,	"
15	Mayflower,	Messrs. Swift, Eldridge, Taylor,	"

Each boat is designated by its number as given above, that the Judges and those witnessing the regatta may at once recognize them.

F. B. Goss, Steam Printer, Barnstable.

Handbill courtesy of John Ehret.

There was a large crowd on the shore and groups could be seen at different points along the shore of the harbor, and on elevated positions about the town. There was also a goodly assembly at the Point, and several visiting yachts were in the harbor.

"The wind was blowing fresh from the north and there were seven boats that started in the first class and seven in the second class. The course laid out for the first class was 14 miles and for the second 11 miles. The gun for the start was fired at 1:11 o'clock and the first class boats passed the line in the following order: *The Olive*, Asa Jones; *Carrie B. Woods*, Charles E. Jenkins; *Fleetwing*, Harry Arey; *Pamona,* Braley Jenkins; *Mayflower*, Swift, Eldridge and Taylor; *Daisy*, W. F. Gorham; *Independence*, Tenny and Haskins. *The Olive* kept the lead until after passing the first stake boat and the *Carrie B. Woods* passed her and kept the lead until she arrived in. The *Pamona* soon after overhauled the *Olive* and all the way up the harbor the two boats kept close together; but when within half a mile of the starting point the *Olive* 'pulled' out of the course and gave up the race, and soon after 'a little puff' brought the *Pamona* home, thereby winning the second prize." The winner's actual time was four hours, five minutes and 51 seconds. Only the first two boats finished, some managed to reach their moorings by rowing (pulling) a bit and others remained at the Point awaiting the next tide. None of the second class made it back so their race was postponed until the following Tuesday. Handicaps were calculated by Loring Crocker, Jr. and Howard Hopkins. The second class race on the following Tuesday covered an 11 mile course and was won by Raymond Hopkins with actual time of one hour, 37 minutes and 59 seconds. Photographs of big cats racing from this period show handsome craft with bowsprits and jibs, unusual touches added for speed. One of the boats has a crew of five and perhaps more, to give a sense of size.

There are several other points of interest about the 1882 regatta. Braley Jenkins, the Sandy Neck cranberry mogul and subject of the next chapter, placed second at age 70. He raced the *Pamona*, the big cat he had built for carting pickers and cranberries to and from the Neck. Herbert Lovell was meant to race his *White Swallow* in the second class but did not make the starting line in time. He and his father, Benjamin, were running the Barnstable Harbor House, their eatery on the Point that served on short-notice. Perhaps it was a case of business before pleasure.

A final paragraph to the original *Patriot* article calls attention to a possible third class race. "As there is a little surplus of cash in the treasury the managers have decided to offer a small cash prize to sailing skiffs, dories, and such like, as a third class. No restrictions as to amount of sail to be carried and no allowances made. All boats start in a line and first boat completing the course takes the money." The race, postponed to the next Tuesday, was won by the *Banner*, Harry Beale, in one hour, five minutes and 30 seconds. Harry Beale, who had just graduated from Harvard College that year, is better known as Joseph Henry Beale, one of the Harvard Law School's most renowned professors. He was also one of the founders of the Barnstable Yacht Club.

By the early 1900s the days of the schooners and big cats had slipped away. Captain Ensign Jerauld, who had a fish market at the end of Freezer road, owned the schooner *Bloomer* which he sailed to the Grand Banks and elsewhere in pursuit of inventory. It was one of the last if not the last working schooner in the Harbor and ultimately may have rotted on shore somewhere near the mouth of Maraspin Creek.

Sailing a big cat in Barnstable Harbor around 1900.

Chapter Seven

BRALEY JENKINS AND HIS CRANBERRIES

The Indians had gone, shore whaling was a thing of the past but one man kept Sandy Neck very much in focus. The natives had enjoyed the Neck's wild cranberries as had the early comers who believed they had medicinal value and warded off scurvy. But Braley Jenkins was one of the first to capitalize on their commercial possibilities.

Born in 1812 he lived in West Barnstable with his father known as Deacon Braley Jenkins (1775-1873) because for 75 years he served as deacon of the West Parish Church. Deacon Braley was a carpenter who built houses in Nantucket and Brewster. He was noted for his hard work and skill and, according to Elizabeth Jenkins in *Three Centuries of a Cape Cod Town*: "…stepped over to Brewster Monday morning for his weeks work and walked back after work Saturday night, earning the regular carpenter's wage of $1.00 per day…" Another local history reports that he worked 14 hour days and that he built a three story house in Nantucket with estimates so precise that after the house was finished there was only a basketful of waste material left.

Son Braley never married, started life as a carpenter but then changed and made farming in West Barnstable his business. His orchards were said to be the best in town. He was a large grower of pears and other fruit, and, according to the *Cape Cod Library of Local History*, stout of figure, slow of movement, scrupulously honest and the first to grow and market "Cape Cod Cranberries". While the successful cultivation of wild cranberries began in the 1840s, years earlier blue water sailors, whalers and others, had learned to appreciate cranberries for their taste and lasting qualities. Early to recognize the wider potential market, Braley created his own bogs in West Barnstable: but, also, the wild cranberry bogs on the Neck had caught his eye. Beginning in 1840 when he was 28 he began to acquire all available interests in the unoccupied stretch of dunes and bogs. After a long string of conveyances he owned or claimed to own much if not most of Sandy Neck. Braley had become an early Cape Cod real estate tycoon.

Between acquisitions he built his large catboat, the *Pamona*, which he used to carry young pickers to and from the Neck and to bring his berries home to market. Elizabeth Jenkins reminisced "The schools changed their calendar, beginning about August 20 for a five week term, then closing until after 'cranberry time' that the boys and girls might earn something for clothes and pocket money. Braley Jenkins ...set to work on the wild bogs of Sandy Neck. Trips back and forth on his craft, *Pamona*, and camping out in 'Braley's House' have never been forgotten by those he chose for pickers."

Antique cranberry scoops and a box for one pound of Cape Cod Cranberries.

Braley died in 1894. Here are quotes from his obituary in the *Patriot*: "Mr. Jenkins was widely known through his connection with the Sandy Neck cranberry. Way back previous to 1850 he quietly bought up all the wild cranberry lands upon Sandy Neck which had previously been considered public property, and at once proceeded to place them in good bearing condition. The shutting out of our people from these bogs caused no little feeling, friction and litigation; but Mr. Jenkins successfully stemmed the tide of public opinion, came out ahead, and for years has been undisturbed in his possessions. He was really the pioneer in cranberry culture in this section. He first introduced the Cape Cod cranberry to the general public, and the Sandy Neck cranberry originally secured for the Cape Cod berry the high standard it still retains. Mr. Jenkins was a very quiet, but, most persevering man, always honorable in his dealings with his fellowmen, and he leaves behind a host of friends. He has always lived on the place he inherited from his father- perhaps the oldest in town..."

The December 23, 1898, *Patriot* noted "The Sandy Neck property owned by the estate of Mr. Braley Jenkins was sold by auction last Thursday to A. D. Makepeace, Esq. for $1505 and a mortgage of $150. This property embraces several cranberry meadows and over two miles of the Bay shore." A thousand acres were supposedly included.

Braley's House is gone now but it was probably back in the dunes adjoining Try Yard Meadow. Whenever we pick the wild bogs with my old scoop we think of Braley and the happy voices of his excited pickers playing in the dunes. The *Pamona* probably docked in the cut next to the Little House. One piling from the old dock still stands in the black marsh bank near where we moor our boat and swim.

Chapter Eight

INTRODUCING THE LITTLE HOUSE

Built against the dunes of Sandy Neck on Try Yard Meadow, the Little House is approaching its 100th birthday. The story goes that it was built as a gunning camp for three young Harvard graduates. Protected from the north by dunes it is close enough to the marsh edge to have weathered hurricanes and withstood surges of wind-driven water from the south. It stands alone from and out of sight of two distant neighboring shacks. Facing south it looks across several hundred yards of high marsh to the Harbor and a mile or so in the distance to mainland Barnstable and Cape Cod. Only when the tide is at its highest does it flood under the building. There are no "improvements".

This is an early and undated photograph from the Whelden Library in West Barnstable. The quaint outdoor toilet arrangement is long gone, a victim of time, weather or good taste.

The Little House is a small (only 12 by 24 feet) one-room, shingled camp designed to hold an unsympathetic nature at bay and to provide that modicum of warmth and congeniality needed to make chilled duck hunters happy. It was built between 1911 and 1914. Today it stands on pilings several feet above the marsh, although the original pilings were nearer marsh level. The narrow covered porch, reached by several steps, runs along the 24 foot southern facade. You step into the single room through a door from the porch and are greeted by a study in compact comfort typical of the hunting camps of the era. Light is from the doorway and three windows. The walls, comprised of studs and exterior sheathing, have mellowed over the years with age and smoke from many fires. A low ceiling helps make for cozy space. The room is snug and inviting in the limited light. The north wall has a table, an overhead shelf, a window and one upper bunk next to the fireplace on the east wall. On both sides of the fireplace mantel are shelves

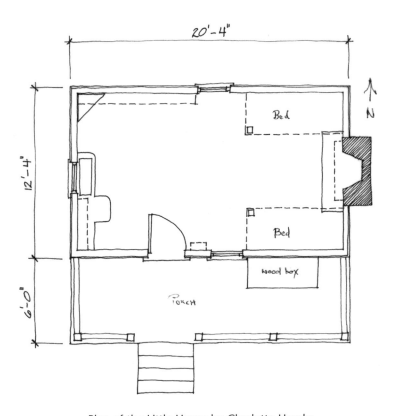

Plan of the Little House by Charlotte Handy.

with odd books that date back to the early days. Next to the fireplace on the south wall is a second upper bunk, another window, the door and a corner where various things lean against the wall. The west wall has dish shelves, its window over a wooden sink that once had a hand pump and a dark corner where the coal stove once stood. It has long since rusted out and been retired with due ceremony. Over the low ceiling is the lightless attic where in the winter mice and better-mannered raccoons play.

There you have it, the Little House, in all its modest splendor. One should add that there are no modern conveniences, only lantern and fire light, hand-carried water and, thankfully, only the barest memories of a telephone. Cell phones have visited but are unwelcome and temporary guests.

Reading the above, it doesn't sound like much: and it isn't. But come evening, looking down from a dune after dinner, the lighted window speaks eloquently to some fundamental need we all share for enough warmth and light to fend off cold and darkness. Standing alone it could be a first shelter, simple but compelling and dearly welcome when needed.

Along with other buildings on the Neck, the Little House is on the National Register of Historic Places. It is probably one of the few surviving Cape Cod gunning camps in close to original condition. The records of the Town's Historical Commission refer to its architectural style as "cottage vernacular" and describe it succinctly as a "...one room cottage (only 12' by 24') ...originally built for use as a gunning camp. Its interior is typical of the cottages in the upland area of Sandy Neck...coal stove, fireplace, bunk beds. A covered porch on the south...overlooks the marshes where migrating waterfowl return to breed and flocks of brant and Canada geese feed along the tidal creeks." In papers supporting its application for recognition of the Sandy Neck camps on the National Register, the local commission referred to the Little House as the "Try-Yard Meadow Cottage".

From time to time, when winter winds reshape the dunes, white crumbly pieces of whalebone turn up behind the Little House, reminders of the old try yard that gave name to Try Yard Meadow.

Chapter Nine

GUNNING

While waterfowl have undoubtedly been shot in Barnstable Harbor since the earliest days, the records are scanty. One of the highest elevations of the mid-Cape moraine south of the Great Marsh is known as Shoot Flying Hill. From there Indians supposedly shot and brought down geese with bows and arrows. Either the Indians were extraordinary shots or geese blackened the sky or both.

The plentitude of water fowl, fish and shellfish in the days of the Pilgrims is hard to imagine.

Mourt's Relation, written in 1621, describes the Pilgrims' first day in Provincetown Harbor, November 11, 1620: "There was the greatest store of fowl that ever we saw. And, every day we saw whales playing hard by us. Of which, in that place, if we had instruments and means to take them; we might have made a very rich return: …"

Edward Winslow, in *Good News from New England*, published in 1624, advised prospective settlers to "Bring every man a musket, or a fowling piece. Let your piece be long in the barrel; and fear not the weight of it, for most of our shooting is from stands…" Stands were props used to steady the guns.

Plymouth Harbor, when they came there on December 16, 1620, they found to be "… a most hopeful place [with an] innumerable store of wild fowl… [full] of fish in their seasons… [with an] abundance of mussels, the greatest and best that we ever saw. Crabs and lobsters, in their time, infinite."

Thomas Morton's *New English Canaan* published in 1637 recalls his visit to New England in 1622. In his opening note to the "Gentle Reader" (using today's spelling) he writes that his purpose is to "…Present to the public view an abstract of New England…" Farther along in the *Second Booke* of his prospectus he tells of "Fowles" in abundance "… I have had often 1000 [geese] before the mouth of my gun. I never saw any in England…so fat…the feathers of them make a bed, softer than any down bed that I have lain on…[there are] black ducks in great abundance…"

Some years later, Governor Bradford, recalling the year 1621, wrote in his history *Of Plymouth Plantation* "All ye somer ther was no wante. And now begane to come in store of foule, as winter approached, of which this place did abound when they came first (but afterward decreased by degrees)."

From these early reports one can extrapolate how plentiful the wildfowl must have been in Barnstable Harbor, blessed as it is with the richly productive Great Marsh. As late as the 1950s, I can remember morning flights of black ducks leaving the Harbor that almost blackened the sky. Certainly the numbers were inspiring and, for me at least, countless.

My father grew up in Barnstable in the early 1900s shooting black ducks by day and on moonlight nights over pot holes. Limits, if they existed at all, were generous and the hunters of his generation were splendid shots. Coot shooting was the real test. The gunners would anchor themselves in a dory at the mouth of the Harbor and drift a string of black-painted canvas bags behind the boat. The locals referred to scoters and probably eider, both big, tough sea ducks, collectively as "coot". There the shooters sat in a bouncing boat in mid-channel visible for miles around and the coot swung by in steady strings. But they came and left at high speed and the shooting could be constant but frustrating. Dad once told me that he had done it for long hours one day with some school friends. He had a ten gauge shot gun and, as the day progressed, his shoulder got increasingly sore. Finally, he began shooting holding the gun against the side planks of their dory. Not designed for this particular kind of maltreatment, the boat soon sprung a leak and the boys were forced to shore, wetter and wiser.

Until the Migratory Bird Treaty of 1918 between the United States and Canada made it illegal, it was fair game to hunt shorebirds. Frederick E. Lowell, Lyman T. Dyer and Joseph Sargent, Jr. had a gunning camp built for them in 1894 deep in the Great Marsh and a mile or so to the west of the Little House. A notebook with seven tattered pages succinctly records several of their trips to the Neck.

The first entry reflects a visit by Messrs. Dyer and Sargent from October 16 through October 23, 1896, and nothing more. On February 22, 1897 a group visited and were apparently too cold or too empty handed to enter anything but initials. From July 31 through

August 2, 1897, two shooters harvested "1 spotted rump, 2 summer yellow legs, a sanderling, a ring neck, small peep. 4000 horse flies." That entry was followed by this quotation "That's all I wish & nothing more." Most people feel differently about horse flies. Four men came between August 23rd and 25th, 1897 and shot "13 sanderling, 16 semi palmated, 1 least, 2 winter, 2 turnstones, 4 summers." Back again for three days in September 1897, the three hunters bagged: on the 2nd, "26 peep, 6 turnstones, 1 black breast and 1 winter"; on the 3rd "4 winter yellowlegs, 7 peep and 21 sanderling"; and on the 4th, "1 winter and 1 summer yellowlegs." A four day visit in January warranted only initials. On October 31, 1898, five shelldrake were shot. Two visited for four days including the first two of 1899, and in cold weather brought in "5 old squaw, 2 shelldrake and 1 whistler." The next entry is for October 13 through 16, 1899. The first day they got "6 gray coot" and noted that birds were not very plentiful. For this and the next day the log recites that they "Saw a few beetle head. Heard a few yellow legs." A five day visit beginning August 8, 1900, netted: "3 beetle head, 26 peep, 2 ring necks, 2 sanderling and 5 summer yellow legs." The final note for this visit reads " No mosquitoes till today. Grub, tobacco & everything else ran out. Millions of mosquitoes at night." The final entry in the log was made on September 12, 1902, and it refers to leaving West Barnstable after driving to Cotuit for keys. The log is in sad shape with missing pages. Based on *Birds of America*, the 1936 edition published by Garden City Publishing Company, Inc., here is a likely translation of the common names the hunters used to currently accepted nomenclature.

Common Name	Bird Book Listing
Spot-rump	Hudsonian Godwit
Summer Yellowlegs	Lesser Yellowlegs
Ring-neck	Semipalmated Plover
Peep	Least or other small sandpiper
Winter Yellowlegs	Greater Yellowlegs
Black breast	Dunlin
Sheldrake	Red-breasted Merganser
Old Squaw	Long-tailed Duck
Whistler	Golden-eye
Gray Coot	Common Scoter
Beetle head	Black-bellied Plover

Since their camp was deep in the Great Marsh, where blacks and geese are the residents, it's surprising that the bags included neither, only one whistler and several scoters, old squaw and sheldrake. This suggests they must have shot well to the east of their house where the water is more open. One wonders whether they moved out into the Harbor by dory or gunning skiffs. Another note of interest is the hudsonian godwit, a lovely shorebird seen annually at Monomoy, rarely elsewhere in the United States and rare today in Barnstable. And note that they were hunting shore birds in late summer and early fall at the height of their migration, some destined as far south as Argentina.

Shorebirds were fair game when my father grew up. He could whistle striking imitations of the calls of yellowlegs and black-bellied plover. Shortly after they were married, he took his new wife shorebird hunting in Barnstable. Her formative years in Ohio hadn't prepared her well for the adventure. I was told that with one shot she got a big haul of peep but I never did hear about a second trip.

Shorebird and duck hunting did generate wonderful decoys. We found in the Little House some crude black duck decoys and, nested together, a half dozen folding metal plover decoys, nicely painted and well preserved considering the proximity of salt water. Unfortunately no early log from there has survived recording visits and takes over the years.

Shorebirds became illegal game in 1918 but not before the Eskimo curlew was thinned out beyond recovery. T. Gilbert Pearson writes in *Birds of America* "In the seventies and early eighties Eskimo Curlews in countless numbers came annually to the coast of Massachusetts…One observer declares that they came in millions that darkened the sky…Tens of thousands thus came to the…beaches of New England where, according to Forbush, they were mercilessly shot for food. Because at this season they were always extremely fat they were known generally as Dough-birds."

Once at Anna Station in north western Australia, several of us participated in cannon netting shorebirds for banding. For a few moments I held in my hand a little curlew said to be very like the Eskimo curlew, now presumed extinct. The little curlew, a bird of the Pacific and Siberia, doesn't pay calls to Barnstable.

There was a period of market gunning in the Harbor when the harvest was shorebirds, duck and geese. Taisto Ranta told me about a market gunner who had a large gauge gun mounted on the front of his boat and would never shoot unless he could be sure of 50 or 60 ducks. A hooked stick down the throat was used to eviscerate the water fowl which were thrown in a barrel and shipped to market in Boston.

Whistler decoy

Dan Knott, a local marine designer, built a special gunning skiff for Marcus Howes, who Dan said "was anyway part duck". Certainly he was one of the best known of the local hunters. I shot with him once with my father when I was twelve or thirteen but I don't remember much except that it was cold. Marcus was said to be a spectacular shot. Taisto was given his gun by a generous Barnstable summer resident. It is a Winchester 12 gauge pump with a full-choke 34 inch barrel, the longest I've ever seen. Remember Winslow's advice about long-barreled fowling pieces. But Marcus did not shoot with a prop under his gun into rafts of swimming birds. He wanted distance for wing shots.

The old Cape Codders who had grown up hunting in Barnstable were good. In the 1940s we had a volunteer fire department and rescue squad. Late one night three shots, a commonly recognized distress signal, were heard at the end of one of the shore roads. They were reported and the rescue squad came but instead of a man in dire straits they found only a pile of black ducks illegally shot after sunset. At the time awed residents said the ducks were all one sex. Because black ducks are hard to sex, I never did believe that part of the story, but the old timers did continue the night shooting they had done as boys, and they could shoot!

Old squaw decoy

PART THREE

Why We Bought The Little House

"The only way to get rid of temptation is to yield to it."
Oscar Wilde, *The Picture of Dorian Gray* (1810).

"I will arise and go now, and go to Innisfree
And a small cabin build there, of clay and wattles made;
. . .
And I shall have some peace there, for peace comes droppng slow,
Dropping from the veils of the morning to where the cricket sings; . . ."
William Butler Yeats, *The Lake Isle of Innisfree* (1890).

The Little House, an oil painting by John Hagen.

39

Chapter Ten

THE INDEPENDENT PROJECT

In 1972 the girls in the senior class at Miss Wheeler's School in Providence, Rhode Island, were assigned an off-campus, independent project. Most did volunteer work of various kinds in or around Providence. Two spunky seventeen-year olds, our daughter Susie and her friend Jenny Kintzing, decided to spend the month on Sandy Neck in the Little House. Their report begins with these words from Thoreau's *Walden*:

"How could youths better learn to live than by at once trying the experiment of living?"

No one had spent more than a night or two in the gunning shack for almost thirty years, not since Lee Austin and Gordon Marshall bought it in 1945 and evicted the squatter couple. Living in the Little House was a sizeable challenge. It had no water, no lights, only a fire place for heat, no toilet, no neighbors, was three miles from a traveled road and almost a mile across the Harbor to the nearest civilization. The girls had a 12 foot tin boat with an engine that worked, usually, but neither girl was a skilled mechanic, nor experienced at sea. May on the Cape can be, and at times that year was, bleak and raw. Taisto Ranta, the Ranger who patrolled Sandy Neck, was the one anchor to windward and he promised to watch over the girls. And they did have a baby raccoon and at times dogs for company. Susie had gotten the raccoon cub in Brewster on April 22 and their stay on the Neck began on April 29 before it opened its eyes to the strange world of a remote gunning camp inhabited by two girls who were just learning to build a fire.

The record confirms that Lee Austin assented to the girls' plan. And parents must have, too, although both sets were plying their respective trades in Providence and could provide no succor except on occasional weekends. It was a brave plan.

These are some of their "Daily observations of the dunes and beach", Sandy Neck in May as seen through the keen eyes of seventeen-year-olds.

May 1 Today we walked around on the dunes in back of the cabin. For the most part, they are covered only with beach grass. The new spikes are already about a foot high... Hudsonia grows in the less exposed areas.

Beach plum bushes are also common. They're covered with buds that look like they should burst any minute. There are lots of bayberry bushes.... Poison ivy thrives out here...we have walked through some that has been up to our shoulders. It grows in huge patches. The leaves are deep red, on top of long single stems. Seaside goldenrod is sprouting new leaves...

May 2 This afternoon we went into the marsh identifying plants. Just in front of the house, if you push aside the mats of dried grass, you can see the new green growth of spartina patens. Walking down towards the water we saw tiny sea lavender leaves; all less than an inch high. The leaves are green and somewhat fleshy, and outlined in red. The glass-wort has just come out of the ground, only the tops of the stalks are visible, and they too are tipped with red. The edges of the creeks are surrounded by dry spartina alterniflora, but we do not see any new shoots yet.

May 3 In a hollow surrounded by dunes we found a patch of wild cranberry....We have seen more of it in the woods, as it thrives in boggy areas....Red winged blackbirds and sparrows spend a great deal of time around the hollow- they must have a nest somewhere nearby.

The raccoon is drinking four ounces of milk a day.

May 4 Today we walked to the parking lot, starting on the inside road (next to the marsh) and cutting across to the back beach at trail #3. It was foggy and because of the moisture the pitch pine trees looked very impressive. Their bark was black and the needles a bright, light green. We saw quite a few holly trees on the inside road... around ten or so.

This afternoon we walked along the back beach. There was a huge amount of seaweed at the high tide level, probably because of yesterday's high winds. The colors ranged from dark green to chartreuse, all shades of brown, and brick red to pink. The shapes varied also; some were long, flat ribbons (three feet by five inches) some bush-like and others in fine filaments.

One type, rockweed, has air bladders on the end of the stems.

We saw a small group of loons swimming around, just a little way offshore...they make a really weird noise, sort of like people laughing.

May 5 On the back beach, the tiny sandpipers were a riot. When a wave receded they would go in a fritz around where the water had been. When the wave started to come back up the beach they'd wait until it was about a half an inch away, and then run so it wouldn't catch them. They look funny running because their legs move so fast.

May 8 Walking across the dunes today we discovered a small group of pussy willows. They were growing on top of a mound of sand, right in the middle of the Neck.... A strange thing to find in such an unprotected place.

Some of the beach plum has started to bloom. Only the branches that are close to the sand level are opening, probably because they're more sheltered.

The raccoon started to open one of her eyes.

May 9 This morning we walked down the road to the east for a while and then cut through to the back beach. The woods are mainly pitch pine, with some scrub oak, blueberry, and bayberry. The pine trees are all twisted and gnarled from the almost constant wind. The wind also keeps them from growing very high- most were under 15 feet. The lower branches grow in all directions, sometimes being buried under sand, then rising out of it some five or six feet away. The floor of the forest is thick pine needles, occasionally interspersed with patches of bearberry.

We passed some boggy areas. Some have cat-tails and phragmites growing in them, others blueberry and other bushes. The water in them is really strange, absolutely black. It is difficult to discern which are a few inches deep, and which a few feet- until an unsuspecting dog or human suddenly finds out! Some had millions of tiny tadpoles living in them.

The raccoon has both eyes open. She is using her hands like a raccoon and has been since about May 6.

May 10 ... On the back beach we passed a dead seal, about four feet long.

May 11 Today we worked on the seaweed in the marsh. The most common seemed to be rockweed, which is found floating in the pools and growing on the banks at the edge of the marsh. Knotted wrack was also very abundant. Sea lettuce is in the pools, as is winged kelp. The main growth throughout the pools seems to be algae rather than seaweed.

Walking through the eastern woods again we crossed huge patches of hudsonia. It seems to grow in clumps, rather than single plants. We had a moss day-found earth stars (really a mushroom), tiny bright red British Soldiers, and reindeer moss.

The scrub oak leaves have just started to open up-they are deep red and have stringy seed pods. The tree shape itself is suggestive of a Japanese print.

May 12 Walking the back flats today we found a lot of sand dollars. The water has been really rough for the past few days, so we assumed they washed ashore...

May 14 Upon returning from our two days in Providence, we noticed how much greener the marsh has gotten. The high tides have probably helped the plants turn green.

Today we discovered a beautiful place in the woods to the east. Walking through the pitch pine trees you suddenly come to a really beautiful clearing. It is very quiet- you can hear only the wind in the trees. The pines are unusually tall (up to 50 feet would be my guess). Right in the middle of the area is a bog with tangled bull briars and poplar trees growing out of it. The poplar trees, which as far as we know aren't common to the rest of the Neck, are so beautiful! The leaves are similar to birch leaves- really bright green, and they shimmer in the breeze. They don't appear to be very old trees, but the bunch of about twenty or thirty trees seems to be doing well. They are probably able to grow in this area because of the unusually well developed soil, and the shelter afforded by the surrounding trees and dunes.

May 15 This morning we passed some deer tracks by the edge of a pool in the dunes. They must have come during the night...

Today we went for a long walk in the rain. We cut through the eastern woods to the back beach, and then came back across west of the big dune behind the house. In the woods we found all sorts of new trees- mostly cedar and juniper.

We jumped a pheasant when we came over the dune from the beach. He was sitting in a big boggy place, filled with bull briars.

The bearberry has blossomed. The flowers are white and bell shaped, edged with pink.

We found a new type of moss we were unable to identify. It's cup shaped stalks were mixed in with the other mosses.

Started to feed the raccoon applesauce. Seems to like it. Also gave her some baby food (rice) with evaporated milk and sugar.

May 17 Susie walked down to a swamp that goes off the road that leads to Sandwich. She walked all around the edge of the swamp, constantly trying to get into the woods that surround it. The woods down there are very different from those to the east of our house. They are almost impossible to walk through because of the bull briars and other heavy undergrowth. At one point she walked by a poison ivy tree whose stem was at least an inch and a half in diameter.

She walked up to the edge of a dune to look at a holly tree and jumped a female duck sitting on a nest of twelve eggs.

The color range of the scrub oak trees is amazing. There can be two trees right next to each other and one will be deep red and the other creamy white. There were even some shades of yellow and green. There was a lot of wild sarsaparilla and sea beach roach growing near the swamp. There were many skunk and deer tracks in the area as well.

May 18 We walked to the point today to use the phone in one of the houses. It was a great walk- forty-five minutes each way. We walked on the beach both ways because the walking is easier out there. At one point the beach couldn't have been more than ten feet wide at high tide.

It was interesting to see the vegetation at the point....There's a great deal of dusty miller, beach pea, and hudsonia there.

Today at low tide I went down to the edge of the marsh and bird watched for a while. The shorebirds were very active out on the flats. As of yet, we haven't mastered identifying the various types of plovers but there are loads of them there. The yellowlegs are really impressive, especially when they fly because they make a great noise. Black-bellied plovers spend a lot of time up in the marsh - in fact, along with the yellowlegs,

45

they are the only shorebirds that do feed on the marsh rather than simply on the flats. Sparrows, red winged blackbirds and crows come to the marsh from the dunes once in a while for nest material.

Herring gulls and terns constantly fly over the marsh, but they never stay for very long. There is a flock of brant living on one of the islands in front of our house.

The other day we had a pair of pintail ducks feeding within twenty yards of our house. We see ducks flying over the marsh quite often, most likely blacks, but again, I'm not sure.

May 21 The glasswort has grown to between two and three inches tall. It is light green, as opposed to the gray-white of last year's growth that has died.

Raccoon has been walking on all fours for about a week. At breakfast she lapped some milk out of a saucer. She is starting to see a little bit- today while she was walking around one of the dogs moved suddenly and she reared back a bit and froze- she seemed to be watching the dogs.

May 22 At about seven thirty we walked down to the Saddle to watch the sunset. It was really beautiful. Officer Ranta has put up a snow fence to keep the sand from blowing away, as there is absolutely no growth at all. While we were sitting watching the sunset a group of black crowned night herons flew right over us. From a distance they looked like crows, but closer up they were much grayer. They make a really weird noise...they quawk (and that's why they are called Quawks). Six of them circled over our heads for about five minutes.

At the foot of the dune, we found a maple tree ... They shouldn't grow very well in the sand. This one was good sized though, probably six feet high. It was more like a bush than a tree, growing sort of like a scrub oak.

The beach plum is in full bloom now-a couple of weeks later than usual on account of the cold spring.

May 24 The visible animal life in the marsh includes mainly water oriented creatures. Fiddler crabs live in holes in the banks of the creeks. When they come out at low tide, you can see swarms of them crawling around searching for food. The male fiddler crab has one huge claw and one small one, while the female has two small ones. The male uses his large claw in mating only. The crabs are really pugnacious, in spite of their size. The males often fight, and frequently lose their larger claws. In this case, a new one grows on the alternate side. Ribbed mussels also live on the banks of the creeks. They grow in the mud, half buried usually, in order to be anchored in. The ribbed mussel is not edible. Snails and minnows and hermit crabs live in the creeks and pools too.

Raccoons come to the marsh for feeding, but because they are nocturnal, we have never seen one...however we have seen lots of tracks.

A general gem about the mosquito control ditches that are dug in the marsh: Mosquitoes breed in the high marsh, where the larvae live on the surface of small pools. There no predators can reach them. The ditches connect the pools and the harbor, thereby bringing in a fresh supply of water twice a day. The fish that are carried in by the tide eat the larvae.

May 28 Our raccoon has started to play for the first time. She has been chewing fingers, hair, and generally messing around.

June 1 Today the Raccoon lapped applesauce out of a bowl for the first time....

Food for the girls for their stay cost $79 "...an average of a little less than $3.00 per day...which included feeding the dogs and raccoon (and guests)." According to their report, here is a typical week's menu:

Saturday
    Breakfast Yogurt, tea and orange juice
    Lunch   Muffin, orange and coke
    Dinner   Hot dogs, salad with blue cheese dressing and mandarin oranges

Sunday
    Breakfast Blueberry muffins and oranges
    Lunch   Deviled ham sandwiches and Kool-Aid
    Dinner   Beef and barley soup, carrots and celery and peanut butter

Monday
    Breakfast Grapefruit and blueberry muffins
    Lunch   Kool-Aid, orange, carrots/celery with peanut butter
    Dinner   Hot dogs, ravioli, tea

Tuesday
    Breakfast Yogurt, grapefruit, tea
    Lunch   Carrots/celery with peanut butter
    Dinner   Cocoa, chicken gumbo soup

Wednesday
    Breakfast Maypo and grapefruit
    Lunch   Oranges and yogurt
    Dinner   Hot dogs, mandarin oranges and bouillon

Thursday
    Breakfast Tea and grapefruit
    Lunch   Yogurt, carrots/celery and peanut butter
    Dinner   Beef stew and pineapple slices

Friday
    Breakfast Maypo, cocoa and oranges
    Lunch   Oranges and yogurt
    Dinner   Hamburger, yogurt and strawberries with a sour cream and sugar dip

The two wrote these separate reports summarizing their experiences.

Jenny Kintzing
June 5, 1972

Philosophical Essay

I feel that our stay on Sandy Neck did me a lot of good. It was a fantastic experience solely because it was so different from my usual life in the city.

It was so nice to be able to go outside at any time and walk, and be completely alone. At first it seems very quiet, then you notice the sounds all around you. But the difference is the kind of sound: not the constant mechanical sound that you unconsciously block out, but the sounds of nature's wind & birds & animals that you have to unblock your city-ears to hear.

It was great to be constantly surrounded by the varied beauty of the Neck, and to have the time to observe whatever struck your fancy at the moment. It wasn't like a nature walk where you have to see how many birds you can find in a day (though we did do that once and it was fun for a day), or a visit to the beach when you just want to lie in the sun, or summer camp when every moment is accounted for. It was simply learning about nature through books and obser-vation, and having time to just go sit in the middle of the forest and look, and think, and see how beautiful and untouched by nature it all is, without having to worry what particular bird or plant makes it so.

I think I gained independence and a greater sense of responsibility from our experience. We were on our own, with nobody to tell us how to spend the food money, when to go to bed, or how to work. I learned to work a Coleman stove & lantern, how to lay a fire in a fireplace and one to grill stuff in the dunes, how to run a motorboat, how to ration food and money, and how to do a thousand other things that I would have let someone with more experience do for me. We had nobody- so we learned. If something went wrong- like the gas line of the motorboat breaking off and

49

spraying us with gasoline one windy, rough and foggy day. We made it finally, holding the line in place & fiddling with the motor which had decided to be temperamental. We made it because we had to, there was nobody to help us, nobody to take the burden of responsibility from us.

On the scholastic side, we learned to make ourselves work without assignments and quizzes. This made learning more enjoyable. The book I read on salt marshes helped me get a fuller view of life there so I could appreciate and understand things that I otherwise wouldn't have noticed: it wasn't work that was due on a certain day.

Sometimes at night it was strange to think that we were the only people on the Neck and we couldn't get to a phone without an hours walk, and the nearest road besides a beach buggy trail was an hour and a half walk. I felt isolated, yet at the same time, strangely safe from the worries of night in the city.

Susie Handy
June 4, 1972

The Results of my Senior Project

My main intention in spending my senior project on Sandy Neck was to sample living in the wilderness…and as I had spent a summer at the Museum of Natural History, I set out to write a paper about the ecology of Sandy Neck.

I started out with very high ideals: we were going to do a brief history of the Neck in order to understand how it had been used in the past. Next we planned to conduct a detailed study of the various areas of the Neck; cataloguing the plants and animals that we had identified. The last section of our paper was to be devoted to planning for the future of Sandy Neck, particularly regarding the possibility of it becoming a wilderness area.

We moved into our house on Saturday, April 29th. The first few days involved cleaning it out, (it hadn't been lived in for years), and exploring the dunes, marshes and woods. The weather went from bad to worse, and we spent a great deal of time reading. We did walk a lot, always trying to identify flowers, grasses, trees, and once in a while, animal tracks.

Our month flew by, and when we came back to Providence to organize our notes we realized how meagerly our intentions had been carried through. We had kept our observations in separate books, and as our paper was to be written jointly, we had a great deal of condensing to do.

Now we have completed our paper, and I am not at all satisfied with it. Our experiment, however, was extremely successful: we lived independently, I raised a baby raccoon, the boat started on the first try almost all of the time, (that may sound insignificant, but it's a great achievement for me because I hate running motors- now I feel fairly confident about it) and the Neck was perfectly beautiful even though we did have only four or five sunny days. Personally, I was thrilled with our project. The paper, that seems to carry all of the weight concerning whether or not we were successful, gives no idea of what we did, how we lived, or what we learned. I did learn some things about plants and birds and living on my own, but the greatest value lies in our living out there, not in any paper that we may write.

… Students should be urged to do unusual things that they will never have the chance to repeat. In my opinion, my project was much more valuable than volunteering in a hospital because I can do that when I'm fifty years old.

My project was also successful because it gave me several ideas about my future. I would really like to spend much more time out on the Neck, simply living for the sake of living- with no paper pressure or anything like that. I'd also like to illustrate a copy of <u>Walden</u> with photographs. In other words, my project has opened many new doors. It will by no means be over when I hand in my paper, but will continue to live with me for a long time.

Still it was a brave plan well accomplished with consequences beyond Susie's wildest dreams.

Chapter Eleven

TEMPTATION

Three years passed, Susie was finishing her third year in college and the Little House had faded into the dim mists of memory. Then in mid-May in 1975 we had a 24th wedding anniversary and no plans. We had not been to the Little House but did remember Susie's adventure and how much she cherished the experience.

Our old friend, Lee Austin, gave us his sympathetic consent and the house key, and questioned our judgment. In due course we loaded our canoe with sleeping bags, fillet, charcoal, champagne and, with great expectations struck out across the Harbor into the unknown. The tide was draining and our departure was a bit later than we innocently scheduled. The paddle was fine until we ran out of water which meant we had to drag the canoe through the shallows and eventually through the inshore mudflats that border the high marsh in front of the house. We managed to get ashore and carry our belongings across 50 yards or more of marsh to the porch and dry land. Then we tried the key in the nice old brass padlock. It didn't work and dusk had joined our party. There we were, lost on a six mile stretch of deserted sand dunes. Retreat was out of the question so we fumbled about and finally found that one of the window bars was not fast so entry was gained and we had our first evening with fillet, champagne and fire light at the Little House.

The next morning we ate breakfast, walked a bit and, when the tide permitted, loaded the canoe and paddled back to the real world. And that's how, following our daughter's lead, we adults discovered the Little House to be a unique and special place deserving at least a corner of our hearts.

One day in 1977, five years after Susie's month on the neck, I was in my Providence office pushing papers around my desk when the telephone rang. There was a curt, business-like Lee Austin, who announced that he and Gordon had decided to sell the gunning camp for $7,000 and that I had one week to make up my mind. Back then we had three boys in school running up big bills and $7,000 seemed an impossible amount to raise over night.

To buy, or not to buy, that was the question and we answered it in the affirmative. Our collective backgrounds with hunting, fishing and Sandy Neck left the family no choice. Today the compelling rationale seems so obviously clear. First, we as a family had spent time on Sandy Neck and cherished every moment; and places to stay had become increasingly rare. Second, the Little House was well-situated for hunting. Third, fishing nearby had often been rewarding. And fourth, it was isolated but convenient. Consistency may be the hobgoblin of small minds, but with life-decisions the promise of renewing old pleasures does brighten future prospects. Bear with a few memoir paragraphs about our earlier camping, fishing and hunting experiences and the joys of solitude can speak softly for themselves.

In the early 1960s I happened upon a derelict canoe whose owner had progressed to bigger things. It was like a doorway to a new world. Once the sticky job of coating it with fiber glass was done, we had a canoe-barge, heavy but ready for all kinds of ventures and maltreatment. Running rapids in the rivers within reach of Providence was a late winter and early spring diversion but then came summer and a renewal of our growing family's love affair with the Cape's sand and salt water. One summer with another family, we loaded our canoe and their boat and struck out for a two week stay on a remote stretch of dunes and beach. It was a great success for children and parents, tenting, swimming, fishing, clamming, exploring and enjoying God's world. We repeated this for a couple of summers and then moved the operation to the end of Sandy Neck. By then our gear had become quite sophisticated with a couple of motor boats added to our armada. While we had the land owner's consent for our tenting safari, there were apparently town regulations against camping and after a week or so the Ranger, Taisto Ranta, then a somewhat unknown quantity, came along and told us that camping was illegal and that we would have to move off the beach and back into the dunes where he couldn't see us. And we did just that.

For the next several years the two families rented a fine house in the cottage colony at the end of Sandy Neck. These were halcyon days with endless fishing and porch sitting to replace the box sitting of our more primitive campsites. There were long days on the then deserted and always spectacular back flats, blueberries to pick and solitary walks exploring the woods and thickets of the Neck. On some of these walks I met brown thrashers, an occasional sparrow hawk, cedar waxwings and, once, a fox wholly unaware of my presence. It was sleeping under a pine bough for shade on a mound blanketed with pine needles. The fishing at hand and the opportunities for exploring Sandy Neck's wilderness were bonds that knit our family closer together.

And fishing was in our blood. Sue had grown up fishing with her father and brothers. She could put a worm on a hook when the younger boys were still squeamish. Meanwhile my father and I explored Cape ponds still-fishing with grass shrimp. We rented a skiff and caught small-mouth bass, perch and, sometimes, a turtle or eel. Some of our bass ran over three pounds, good fish for those days at least.

When I was 11 and 12 we summered in North Harwich, then a rural village in the mostly untouched middle of Cape Cod. Just off Depot Street there was a culvert where the Herring River flowed under the railroad track on its way to what we called Swan Pond. There was the wonder of looking down on slow-moving water just a few feet below, water teeming with fish. In the spring, the herring ran so thick you could "walk on their backs" the locals said, but I never tried. Occasionally a two foot snapping turtle would drift by rowing slowly to help the gentle current.

Once two of us fished the culvert itself. I had a big square net weighted at the bottom and my cohort had a fearless heart. He walked through the 50 to 75 foot dark tunnel under the tracks driving the fish and other unknowns into my waiting net. Lifting its corners I would work down the embankment to the small beach and we would harvest the catch of pickerel, perch, bull head, "punkin seed" and other miscellaneous critters. Somewhere there's a Brownie picture of one of our splendid catches with two proud boys.

One day a big pickerel lay gently finning just outside the culvert and almost within reach. He must have been at least a yard long, certainly bigger than any fish I'd ever seen. Looking down, I dangled a hook baited with a clam just in front of his long nose wiggling it, making it as tempting as possible. After a bit he mouthed it and spit out the clamless hook, ridding himself of a nuisance and nearly breaking my heart. He and I were both back the next morning and I dropped him a small, hooked perch for breakfast. There the temptation was too much and he struck and ran with the perch across the pool bending double my old metal fly rod until he let go and swam off leaving only my thumping heart to break the silence of the pool.

Herring River, just beyond the culvert under the railroad track, taught me how special a place could be and capped off my addiction to fishing.

My own hunting in Barnstable began early in 1940 when I was eleven. I had a Harrington & Richardson single shot 410, good for rabbits and a rare, close-in shot at a duck or pheasant. Barnstable was still undeveloped then and there were many open fields available for hunting. And that is just what I did in my free time. I was in the seventh grade and the school was in Hyannis, some seven or eight miles away. The school bus picked us up around 7:00 in the morning and brought us home late in the afternoon if we played sports. The bus was driven by an older man named Free Ellis who was firm and commanded respect. Early one Saturday morning when I was traipsing the fields, I met Free rabbit hunting with his 13 inch beagle hound, Peaches, of whom he was enormously proud with good reason. He asked me to join him and put me in a spot with a view through the brush where he expected the rabbit to come. And it did and I got my first bunny for Free's soup pot. Actually he generally ate rabbit pie. He loved his rabbit hunting but had a bit of trouble hearing the bunnies hop into range so he came to depend on me to fill his larder. While his hearing was less than perfect he could still scramble through and over the bushes at a rate that kept me quiet and panting. One of us or sometimes Peaches would jump a rabbit and Peaches would pick up the scent and follow the bunny at the very slow pace that kept it from holing up. Eventually it would circle back to its starting place and, "when it was in your face and eyes" as Free would say, it became fair game. Those were great days for men, boys and dogs.

On some Saturdays I would shoot ducks with my father. Mostly we shot on Nine Mile Pond from a point where in earlier days flyers had been used to bring wild ducks and geese into range. This hunting tech-

Goose decoy by Joseph Lincoln.
Photograph courtesy of Theodore Harmon.

nique, like corning, was illegal by the time I started but we did hunt over some wonderful goose decoys carved by Joe Lincoln. One in perfect paint was auctioned off recently with an estimated price of $25,000 to $35,000. We shot enough for me to realize what a fine wing shot Dad was and how unlikely it was that I would ever become one with our two or three bird limit. We often hunted there with Laury Mortimer, a depression victim who returned to the Cape from Wall Street and turned native. One morning it was still dark when we stopped to pick him up. He had overslept and asked us in to join him while he had a quick breakfast. We did and he

tossed down a tumbler of whiskey. Men were men in those days and this eleven year old was duly impressed. Laury was a good soul and that Christmas he went off to Long Island to shoot with friends. Several days before Santa was expected I got a large cardboard box in the mail from New York and Laury. I brought it home and opened it and there was a limp, fresh- ly shot snowy owl. While the poor owl had my sympathy, it did get stuffed and was a treasured possession for many years.

Driven by these memories, the family decision to purchase the Little House was preordained and so it came to pass.

Jeb with his first bluefish.

56

Chapter Twelve

THE LEARNING CURVE

So in 1977 the Little House became a family affair, situate in a place rich in history and beauty. How would we protect and use it in our modern world and harvest its rare potential?

No one in the family except Sue knew anything about the purchase and Christmas was drawing near. In my basement shop I managed to create a passable 10 inch replica of the building with porch, steps, impressionistic shingles, windows and door, all lilliputian in scale but recognizable to anyone who knew the structure. It was nested tenderly in a good-sized box packed around with tissue paper and then carefully and handsomely wrapped by Sue, a genius at such things. To the package was appended a piece of white cardboard with a picture of an Eskimo curlew and the following in red ink:

RIDDLE-1977 et seq

I stand alone, alien
At the outer edge
A quiet corner
Out of the world's way.

Refuge of mice and men,
My neighbors are fowl.

I am a fragile outpost.
My gray bones are brittle.
Hold me tender.

I have been loved and
Left out in the cold.
But I endure
One of a kind.
Beautiful and old.

Well, of course, Christmas being what it is, all hustle and bustle, with children ranging from 10 to 20, no one solved the riddle or probably even tried. The package was opened, there were squeals of delight and, for a moment, there were probably visions of sand dunes instead of sugar plums, then attention shifted to other packages. One bore an important relation to this writing. It was from our close friend, George Warren, who anticipated how much the house would come to mean to all of us better than we did. He was a romantic with a passion for wild, out-of-the-way places and his present was a haunting painting of the Little House done by Anne Packard. This was one of her earliest: since then she has become widely acclaimed. For George, who enjoyed Anne's company, giving the picture away was like parting with a hand and no present has ever been as treasured or meant more to our family.

Anne Packard's painting of the Little House.

We all survived that memorable Christmas day and the next day brought the first entry to our house log:

1977 Senior Handys, Susie and Seth and George and June Warren walked out the first day after Christmas. First look.

Not much, but it was probably too cold for lavish praise and certainly too late for cold feet. And real love grows slow.

Over the years we have learned about the recurring concerns and delights of a remote getaway and some are depicted here with script entries from the log for reality. Today being a wet, raw March day on Cape Cod, how nice to think of a summer visit to the Little House with attendant pleasures and problems.

The threshold question is how to get there and there are various possibilities. Walking is an hour and a half or more of drudgery in the sand. It's a four or five mile drive down the back beach and over the dunes taking a good part of an hour. There is an access road that brushes against the house but somehow driving down Sandy Neck's wild back beach and across the Neck through the silent and almost virgin pine forest seemed discordant with the peace and quiet of the Little House. From the beginning we decided no driving. The practical approach is by boat timed to suit the tides. Early trips were generally by canoe and later by kayak, a pleasant 15 or 20 minute paddle in good conditions often with wayside views of birds, surfacing fish or, rarely, seals to break the repeating splash and drip of the paddles.

Paddled by a Merganser sitting on a piece of caved marsh bank...within six feet, both equally surprised-he at seeing an eskimo kayak this far south and me at seeing a Merganser here in July

Time being incidental, we often stop to catch a fish or tread up a quahog or two for dinner. The tide, of course, is always a factor. At times we have run out of water and had to drag the canoes across sand and mud flats a quarter of a mile or so, considered by visiting friends a serious breach of promised relaxation.

Once there your boat has to be made fast. Not a problem with a canoe but as size, capacity and weight increase, so added care becomes necessary. One night Sue and I had sailed over in our 14 foot catboat, the *Bay Bird*. When we awoke in the morning it was blowing hard from the north and we were boatless. A high-course tide and a too short anchor line had given the *Bay Bird* a chance to kick up her heels and drift off on her own. After walking several miles to civilization, we called for help and later found our boat comfortably beached, safe and sound somewhat east on the Barnstable side of the Harbor. The other risk to consider when mooring is the possibility at flood tide of one's boat being blown over the high marsh and, when the tide ebbs, being found there high and dry. There it would stay until the next equal tide, possibly a long wait for a heavy boat dropped there by unusually high water. Over the years many innocents have had an unexpectedly long rest due to an anchor dropped in the wrong place.

The next challenge is climbing the slippery marsh bank to where the footing is less like banana peels and the path to the house is negotiable, more or less. Walking becomes more exciting after dark. Years ago an earlier owner had dug out a small pot hole to sit in for duck shooting. This, a drainage ditch, a big natural pothole and a mosquito ditch along the path warn visitors to travel with care. There have been many dips and soakings at this stage of the visit replete with laughter and, sometimes, even expletives.

There are other seasonal and occasional landing hazards. On a windless day, especially early or late, no-see-ums lay claim to the shore's edge and the trick is to cover the hundred plus yards to the porch as quickly as possible. Fortunately this is not a common menace. The porch is a sanctuary, perhaps because it is farther from the shore and closer to the dunes or perhaps because of its elevation.

Notwithstanding these modest problems, each visit drew us closer to a way of life far removed from the busy hum of men.

From day one there was the grim specter of upkeep. Gordon Marshall, our wise predecessor in title, advised us to avoid improvements that might tempt vandals. Easy advice to follow, and follow it we did. Problems surfaced immediately. The sash in the three windows either wouldn't open or wouldn't stay up because of uncooperative window weights. Solving this, because of the necessary planning and the technical challenge, took many restful hours. We did have to evict the mice that had chewed off the ropes or had built their clogging nests around the weights but our advance in knowledge about how window weights really worked, in addition to being able to open and close the windows, made the investment of time worth while.

Most of the furniture had served many years and was tired. Some of the replacements were worse.

Lost another round with my bargain captain's chair - it let me down.

We did install temporary tables that hung over the marsh from the porch railing made from old, rejected window shutters that, along with other debris, came with the house. The antique coal stove in one corner was rusted out and an obvious fire hazard. Its smoke had exited through a rusted stove pipe to a stub brick chimney that poked out of the roof at the west end of the house. When we evicted the stove, the stove pipe went too.

Debris from the stove pipe contained 10 or 12 prehistoric bird skeletons...little ones that didn't make it. Must wire over the chimney.

The stub chimney hanging between roof boards continued to be an irritant.

The west chimney wiggles and should be tended to, sometime. Nude couple in dunes more interesting & a nap.

Following Gordon's advice we let nature take its course and after a couple of winters the useless chimney blew off and a small roof patch solved the problem.

A great storm in January of 1987 did shake us out of our lethargy. Our first daytime post-storm visit revealed

Floor boards upended and resting on upset furniture. Tool chest tipped over & everything all over the place - bunks drenched and mildewed...

But the real damage was more structural and warranted professional help. The house was tipping rakishly weighted down by its surviving chimney rooted in the sand by a sizeable cement foundation. When high tides liquified the sand not surprisingly the chimney structure tended to sink pulling the house with it. It was clearly desirable to elevate the building above high tide level and to rebuild the chimney. In due course after the required permitting this was done assuring survival of the Little House through many more storms, we trust.

Right now the two of them are brainstorming about how to make this an even better place. This kind of conversations seem to be pretty frequent but they rarely come to much - hard to improve on the simple luxury!!

What better argument could be made for deferred maintenance?

After settling in, opening the storm door and window shutters and bringing chairs out to the porch, what then? Usually in the dog days when the tide and temperature are right we've had a cool swim after mooring the boats. The Harbor water often reaches the 70s but always is refreshing and clear unlike the warmer water on the south side of the Cape. Then we often have a walk, sometimes a long one over the dunes, through the woods and out to the back beach. Sometimes on these walks we'll see a deer or fox. Once we jumped a great horned owl which flew ahead in short spurts from pine to pine as we progressed. The pine woods are silent, in many areas free of underbrush and almost always free of other human visitors. Walking there you are your own company alone with your thoughts in a quiet wilderness.

Other options are a fishing run or a several mile sail up into the Great Marsh or out to the Point, all weather dependent. Our fishing now is generally with fly or light spinning rods using home-tied bucktails or home turned popping plugs. Our boys, the real fishermen, like Sluggos, large, heavy-bodied plastic worms, maggot-white, hard to cast, boring to use and to the bass and blues, irresistible. In the early days of our tenure we could keep small school bass and fillets from several of them were a special treat. The little people have their own agendas: tumbling in the dunes, imagine a 60 foot pile of sand to climb and somersault down; or playing their latest game like Frisbee golf. One grandchild has taken to exploring in search of new places and things in this wild wonderland: new things like Indian middens freshly blown clear by the wind or other momentous finds from other times like bits of whale bone or the rusty smoke bombs dropped from planes practicing for more serious duty in World War II.

And then there's always porch sitting and just looking at the passing world perhaps with a book in one's lap for effect or a piece of paper for listing projects that once listed are gone forever. Porch sitting is an art discussed later. With most New Englanders it conjures up uncomfortable feelings of guilt, but with careful disregard such feelings can be dispelled and supplanted by an almost peaceful state of meditation called, in its extreme form, sleep. William Butler Yeats was right when he wrote in *The Lake Isle of Innisfree* "...for peace comes dropping slow..." but the important thing is that it does come.

Busy arranging world affairs from our
contemplative chairs on porch.

Talk centered on naps. Found it soporific.

How nice to live by the tides.

So nice to have time stand still as it does here.
No amount of fussing seems to hurry the tides.

So nice that there's plenty to do here; and that
doing nothing is one of them.

We are here for a serious power nap & reading
books on the porch -- bliss! Ah... dozing off for
an hour in the sun & the wind & air was sheer heaven.

Early on we discovered that near the Little House there was more to harvest than clams. In late August and early September beach plums ripen. They are an unpredictable crop but in good years a half pail is a reasonable take. Often you have to brave poison ivy and the bushes themselves are close-cropped with stout and painfully sharp branches. The fruit is coveted by other residents of the Neck and if we arrive too late we find the ground covered with pits and no sweet blueberry-blue plums. If successful with a little more work we have beach plum jelly, a world-class treat.

The cranberry bogs on the Neck caught the interest of Braley Jenkins and ours, too. The berries ripen in late September or early October. We pick with a scoop I bought as a boy when we summered in rural North Harwich. A friend's father operated several bogs and ran a cranberry screen house on Depot Street where the berries were sorted. He humored me as an eleven year old allowing me to pick with the Portuguese who were lightning fast and impressive. In those days the crop was picked dry then the bogs were flooded to get the "floaters" not considered as desirable. Most berries now are dislodged from the vines mechanically and harvested as floaters but not on the wild bogs of Sandy Neck where the old primitive technique still prevails. For us the cranberries that survive Thanksgiving and Christmas last in the ice-box through the winter and are available for rhubarb pies and other treats.

Sue's Rhubarb, Custard and Cranberry Pie

Beat three eggs

Add three tablespoons milk

Stir in

> One cup sugar
> Four tablespoons of flour
> 1/4 teaspoon of nutmeg

Mix in

> Three cups rhubarb
> One cup of cranberries

Crumb crust to spread on top

> 1/2 cup sugar
> 1/2 cup flour
> 1/4 cup butter

Cook in a 400 degree oven for 50 minutes

There are blueberries on the Neck but very few will say where. Like any treasure hunt, finding the treasure is part of the reward.

Having found this little bit of heaven, what could be better than sharing it with friends. In the hustle and bustle of our daily world, what a rare delight it is to sit with old friends and talk in a place where the reigning silence is broken only by bird songs and the sounds of wind and distant waves. In the many years we've shared this pleasure with others no momentous conclusions have been reached about anything; but somehow a bit more life has been squeezed out of precious minutes. A related joy is sharing the beauties of the woods, dunes and marsh. The Little House sits in a pocket wilderness within sight of civilization but far beyond reach of the ordinary. Visitors new and old leave with a revived sense of wonder. This is recreation at its best. Even Sir Oracle would be muted looking across acres of salt meadows and pastel tinted dunes to the setting sun.

Mornings, evenings and star-studded nights are all wonderful. When we sleep on the porch the mosquitoes come early forcing a pulled-up sleeping bag and, perhaps, one more spray of bug juice. As the day warms the bugs go off about their other business, and we can look down the Neck to the rising sun and watch the light change on the dunes and marsh. Breakfast is usually a quick cup of tea or coffee heated on the Coleman stove, a bit of juice, perhaps some fruit and toast and then clean-up. Often an early departure is necessary to avoid being high and dry for the balance of the day.

Evenings are the special times, often shared with friends. For starters there's the ceremonial drink often at a dune top watching the sun slowly sink into the horizon of distant pines. Then the relaxed stroll back to the porch for hors d'oeuvres (cherry stones grilled open with butter and lemon are delicious), a second drink and then easy good talk. Being so close on the small porch at such an elevated level makes for good company and high-minded talk.

The grill is going, ready for hamburgers and hot dogs (tasty delights in the cool of evening), or steak or mussels or some exotic creation made specially for the treasured outing. And finally perhaps there's a song or poem, a bit of cleaning up and we're homeward bound or ready for sleep. Skunks walk the wrack at night and mosquitoes patrol the marsh edge so we give them each their due.

The trips back to the Yacht Club or Marina after dark always have their little thrills. First there's the question of getting to the boats without discovering an unwanted pot hole. As mentioned above the shore line where we moor our transportation is riddled with shallow trenches, a dug out hole or two, some narrow footing and one wee tidal inlet. A flashlight helps but often the trip is enlivened with squeals and splashes. Sometimes when we've sailed we're blessed with moonlight, a warm gentle breeze and a cooperative high tide and the evening at sea ends with a fine sail home. Those are the nights we choose to remember best.

Homeward voyages are not always so tranquil. One day a visitor asked to sail the *Bay Bird* back to the Yacht Club, a little over a mile perhaps. Included in his cargo was a camera and boom box. Cat boats are stable but the south west wind was lively with little enthusiastic gusts and our intrepid friend tried a sporty jibe which didn't work. We did manage to right the boat and bail it out. Memories of parts of the camera and boom box spread across our back yard to dry still persist. The salvage efforts were unsuccessful and bright little chards of modern technology joined the ranks of other sea victims. Once when canoes had been the craft of choice, a gusty morning wind warned against a return paddle. Then we walked back along the Neck and retrieved the canoes later. Another time we waited until the tide was low, the flats exposed breakwaters and then we towed the loaded canoes back along the bar edges until we were close enough to the lee shore to brave a quick paddle.

It would be wrong to leave Sandy Neck without paying tribute to its insects. One log entry refers to the Neck as *"bug heaven"*: all wrong except, perhaps, for dead ones. First to claim attention are the no-see-ums that meet you at the water's edge and sometimes even in the dunes. Another log entry tells of *"the million mite march"*, another overstated reference to no-see-ums. These pests, a phenomena of windless moments, are swept away by a bit of breeze. Public enemy number two is the horsefly or greenhead. The reference to *"tons of horseflies"* is another exaggeration. They do make themselves known when they bite and they can leave a lasting itch. Greenheads are particularly vicious after a swim, apparently favoring a pinch of salt with their meal. They come in July and are supposed to vanish with the first full moon in August, but some never get the word and linger on for a final chew.

A gentle wind wafted us across the Harbor and we ate lunch & killed horseflies.

No matter what people say, salt marsh mosquitoes are not as big as birds. They are noisy and capable of inflicting lasting bites. They operate mostly in the evening and early morning hours and seem to respect most insect sprays, to some extent. Unfortunately they populate the woods and, in their regular operating hours, the dunes, but are nothing that a strong man with quick hands can't stand. There are wood ticks but only in out of the way places where dogs tend to explore. On the good side are the "noisy" crickets of late summer. They inhabit the windrows of salt hay deposited at the marsh edge by the high tides.

We spent the night on the porch, lulled to sleep by the gentle chirping of millions of cricket musicians, filling the night with their lullabies.

Weather and bugs to the contrary notwithstanding, a day in the outdoors restores the joy of living.

Watercolor of the Little House by Robert Mesrop.

PART FOUR

A Passing Parade

They never came back!
They never came back!
They never came back to me!

Edward Lear, *Calico Pie*

Extinction is forever.

John James Audubon's Eskimo curlews once abundant now believed extinct.
They followed the passenger pigeon as a favorite table delicacy.

Chapter Thirteen

A GRAND CLAM

Soft-shell clams (Mya Arenaria) were a food staple for the local Indians and pilgrims. Numerous shell heaps on the Neck testify to the former and Elder Brewster is said to have complained in other than pious language about his too steady diet of clams. In the late winter and early spring the slow moving clam was easier to catch than birds on the wing and fleet-footed denizens of the forests. We discovered that in our early days of camping east of Sandy Neck. In short order we could dig a pot full, steam them in salt water and dipped in melted butter they made a scrumptious meal.

While we have never tried one at the Little House, clam bakes have always been a local favorite. The boys did try a pig roast once before one of their weddings but, fortunately at the very last minute, all pigs pleaded previous engagements and hamburger had to suffice.

In 1862 Lt. P. de Broca reported to the French government:

"In Rhode Island and Massachusetts clams serve as a pretext for fetes of a very peculiar kind called Clam-Bakes. The clam-bakes have their origin in an old Indian custom.

The aborigines of these States were accustomed to assemble in great numbers every year for feasts consisting of clams and green corn cooked with sea-weed…. These feasts are delicious beyond description, and it is said that no one is ever made ill by them. In former times the most renowned warriors came from afar to take part in them, and now they are attended by persons of the highest social standing, sometimes to the number of several hundreds."

Our old and fragile copy of *The Boston Cook Book* by Mrs. D. A. Lincoln with its preface dated 1884 paints this pleasant picture.

"An impromptu clam bake may be had at any time at low tide along the coast where clams are found. If you wish to have genuine fun, and know what an appetite one can have for the bivalves, make up a pleasant party and dig for the clams yourselves. A short thick dress, shade hat, rubber boots, or, better still, no boots at all, if you can bring your mind to the comfort of bare feet, a small garden trowel, a fork, and a basket, and you are ready."

After telling how the bake should be conducted, she continues:

"Peep in occasionally at those around the edge. When the shells are open, the clams are done. They are delicious eaten from the shell, with no other sauce than their own briny sweetness. Melted butter, pepper, and vinegar should be ready for those who wish them; then all may 'fall to'. Fingers must be used. A Rhode Islander would laugh at anyone trying to use a knife or fork."

Cape Cod clam bake around 1900.

The "steamers" of Barnstable Harbor, I heard as a child, were the best in the world. Maybe this was just an excess of local pride but, beginning in the early 1900s, they did provide a major source of income for many of West Barnstable's Finnish families. They could dig at low tide and farm when the flats were covered. In the 1920s there were more than a hundred commercial clam diggers working the flats. The clams were plentiful and the take unlimited. But, as time would show, the supply was not limitless.

Taisto Ranta remembers that around 1936 when he was 16 he joined two West Barnstable men, Francis Atwood and Henry Lampi, and the three rowed their dory with the tide from Scudder Lane over two miles to a bar called the Nubbles just east of Mussel Point. He was allowed two hods, while the adults were allowed and dug four each. Then they rowed back with the incoming tide; Henry pulling alone in the front and Taisto and Francis with one oar each in the back. He remembers Henry saying "Pull, boy, pull. You're not here on school vacation." Taisto got 50 cents a hod his first year and 80 cents the next while the adults got a dollar.

Depending on your authority, it took 4 1/2 or 5 hods to fill a barrel. Working two tides one day Frank Maki is said to have dug seven barrels of clams. According to an unpublished paper by Frederick Atwood at the Whelden Library in West Barnstable "Tauno and Reino Lampi once when digging clams wondered how long it took to dig a hod of clams (the clams being so abundant); timed the effort and it took a little over three minutes to dig each hod full. That would equal 16 minutes a barrel per man".

The same paper describes an experience of John Atwood, then 14, and William Wirtanen, 41, one day in 1922. "John harvested 3 barrels and 2 hods of clams. (4 1/2 hods equal a barrel; a hod holds about 2/3rds of a bushel and weighs 55 lbs. when full.) William harvested 5 barrels. The boat was laden so deeply that there were only a few inches of freeboard. On the way back, a windstorm arose. William was doing the rowing and he was a tremendously strong man. Sometimes he would have to row with one oar so hard that John was sure it would break, because it bent so much. William would count the number of small waves between the large ones and could predict what was going to happen. As the large waves became more frequent and the wind blew more strongly, John became alarmed and took off his hip boots in case he had to swim. William was as cool as a cucumber, but he must have had some apprehension because he began to sing hymns. The worse the storm became, the louder he sang and every once-in-a-while he would spit. He couldn't turn his head to look where he was going, because if he took the time to do it, he couldn't keep the boat headed properly in the waves. He predicted exactly when the waves would abate and told John not to worry; the worst is over. John couldn't see any change and was still worried, but William was correct and they got ashore safely. John wondered why William had done all that spitting. Later he found out that William was judging the wind by the direction of the flying spittle, because he dared not take time to look around."

A Cape Cod dory made by Shirley Lovell.
It measures 17 1/2 feet long with a five foot beam.
This is the type of boat formerly used by clammers in the Harbor.

So clam digging was not without its dangers and at times the briny deep could pose a frightening threat. Some were not as lucky as Atwood and Wirtanen. In 1905 clam diggers, Joe Enos and Jason Amaral, were drowned when their boat swamped about 200 feet from the shore in the Barnstable Harbor channel. Enos could swim and got within 100 feet of shore but, weighed down by heavy clothing, became exhausted and sank. A third man in the boat was rescued. According to the November 25, 1905, *Patriot* "There was a strong northwesterly wind that kicked up a choppy sea and the boat with the three men began to ship water. They had nothing aboard to bail it out, but thought they could reach the shore. Suddenly the boat filled with water and sank beneath them throwing all into the sea. Enos was about 22 years of age and leaves a bride of a month. Amaral, who was drowned, leaves a wife and eight children."

Ernest G. Dottridge became Clam Warden in 1927 and reported that over 16,000 barrels of clams had been taken in 1926 and he warned "We conferred with some of the best informed men and also men who have worked in and known the business for years. They all agree that unless something is done, the flats in Barnstable which supply work for about a hundred men in winter will, in the near future, become exhausted." In his 1928 report he added "The supply in Barnstable is growing less every year on account of the large number of men working and no new set…the amount dug has gone from 50,000 barrels in 1918 to 5,000 in 1928."

The problem was well recognized, and early in the 1900s biologists from the federal and state governments began studying the clam and searching for solutions. Encouraging the establishment of farms to grow clams offered the best promise and Massachusetts adopted legislation authorizing grants of tracts to individuals for clam culture. The idea of privatizing what had been a public right met strong resistance and the few grants made were revoked under pressure from individual diggers. And clam takes continued to decline while prices climbed to record heights.

The biologists had learned that a single female clam releases millions of eggs of microscopic size which when fertilized develop into swimming larva that drift about for a couple of weeks in a world filled with hazards. Survivors then settle into the bottom where, if fortunate, they avoid a host of predators including horseshoe crabs, boring snails and an exploding population of green crabs. Armed with this information, and beginning after World War II, Woods Hole Oceanographic Institution under contract with the Massachusetts Division of Marine Fisheries undertook to study and improve the farming of clams, working particularly in Barnstable Harbor.

Alfred Redfield, the Harvard/ Woods Hole scientist who had grown up in Barnstable sailing the Harbor and shooting with Henry Kittredge, went to work on the flats. Armed with a hand plow and shovel and teamed with his old acquaintance Marcus Howes, the two set out to find answers. Harry J. Turner, in an article entitled *Clams* from an unknown source, notes that the scientist's assumption that the quality of the bedding sediment played an important role in survival "...was bolstered by the report of an old fisherman in Barnstable who claimed to have brought about the settlement of a large number of clams on his grant by resurfacing the area with sediments excavated from a certain marsh bank." The old fisherman was presumably Marcus Howes, said in his obituary to have been well known for the propagation of shellfish. Tom Marcotti, the Town's current shellfish biologist, recently inspected extensive flats to assure that they were unproductive, a requirement if a grant is to be licensed. When he came to the grant worked by Marcus Howes and Alfred Redfield years earlier he found a dense set of clam shells, presumably planted by the two, clams that had lived out their lives undisturbed. It's interesting to think about the long-time friends, the scientist and the old fisherman, working together on the Barnstable flats to learn about growing clams.

The Woods Hole studies continued for ten years and resulted in ten reports written between 1948 and 1958 submitted to the Massachusetts Division of Marine Fisheries and in six other papers published in scientific journals. Turner's article *Clams* summarizes the work and concludes " Now after more than ten years of intensive research it has become clear that the problems associated with the development of clam farming are many and complicated."

Bringing the story up to date, the reported commercial harvest of soft-shell clams has not returned to anything like the levels of the early 1900s. Dottridge reported 50,000 barrels dug in 1918. There were good sets in 1992 when 12,306 bushels were taken and in 1995 when the take was 11,175 bushels. Those numbers tailed off to 403 bushels in 2001 increasing to 1,072 in 2004. A bushel is roughly 1/4th of a barrel so the 1,072 bushels translate to 262 barrels compared to the 50,000 dug in 1918.

And growing soft shell clams on Barnstable's 100 acres of licensed grants has added little. They are perishable and favored by many predators. Nevertheless in 2003 several soft shell clam farmers reported producing approximately 45 barrels valued at just over $13,000.

The crop, which has always been cyclical, still has problems, old and new. Steps have been taken to control over-fishing. Commercial and recreational permits are now required and separate areas in the Harbor are set aside for commercial and recreational digging. In the big years in the 1990s there were almost 200 commercial permits and over-digging resulted. Pursuant to a change of policy the number of permits has, through attrition, fallen to slightly less than 50, the level that policy makers believe will strike a balance between the size of the crop and the potential for earning a decent living. In addition to over-fishing, there are new predators and more pollution. The green crab, a European native, has proliferated.

A commercial permit to dig costs $500 and covers all species of shellfish. The holders value the crop and are said to be self-policing to protect their own livelihoods. And being good Cape Codders, they can go to amusing lengths to protect their own interests. There has been a good set recently, first discovered by a few permit holders who took precautions to cover their tracks and camouflage their trips in and out. A fishing rod was always visible, never a clam rake.

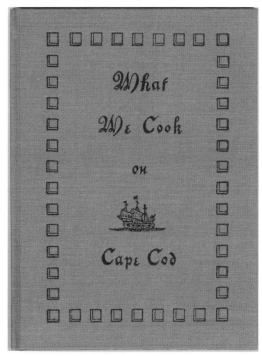

So some things never change, like the taste of good steamed clams or a good clam chowder and here's a traditional recipe from *What We Cook on Cape Cod*, my grandmother's 1911 cookbook:

Cape Cod Clam Chowder. One quart of clams, thoroughly cleaned. One quart of milk, one good sized onion, six potatoes, four slices of pork, one tablespoon of butter, three hard crackers, broken, pepper. Fry out the pork and then put in the sliced onion and cook a few minutes; put them into a large kettle and add the sliced potatoes; boil them till soft in water to cover them; add the clam water (after straining), then the clams. Cook five minutes, then add the quart of milk and when it comes to a boil add butter, cracker and pepper. Enough for six or eight persons. [Mrs. E. D. Crocker]

Joe Lincoln wrote in his foreword to the cookbook

A Cape Cod cookbook! My, oh my!
I know that twinkle in your eye,
And why you're pricking up your ears,
You've turned the clock back thirty years.
I know that smile of yours; it tells
Of chowder, luscious as it smells;
And when you laugh aloud, you dream
Of berry dumpling, bathed in cream.

Chapter Fourteen

COMMERCIAL FISHING

In the 1940s there were five or six fish trap boats working out of the Marina in Barnstable Harbor, continuing a tradition that had begun before World War II and thrived afterwards…for a time.

In 1944 I joined the crew of Mike Goulart and Adam Rumpkis seeking money, adventure and muscle for football. Our boat was 40 feet plus or minus with an open hold, a powerful engine and six hands. It was designed for weir or trap fishing. Our two weirs were located in Cape Cod Bay, along the Sandy Neck shore a mile or so west of the Point.

Each fish trap consisted of three components. First, a *leader*, a net with large mesh dropped to the bottom and stretched on hickory poles 1200 yards from near shore out into deep water. Most fish would see the wall of net and swim out to deeper water to avoid it. Next came the *heart*, a heart-shaped pair of nets of heavier, smaller mesh that, leaving 20 foot or so openings on both sides of the leader, overlapped it at its seaward end. The two pieces of the heart, one on each side of the leader end, ballooned out and closed at their other end at the gate, the entrance to the *bowl*, the third component. The gate when down allowed the fish and the boat to enter the bowl. When the boat was half in the bowl, the gate was snugged up to the boat's bottom and then, when the boat was entirely in the bowl, the gate was pulled up above the surface and the fish were trapped.

The bowl, a small gauge, heavy mesh net, was circular, large enough to contain a 40 foot boat, deep enough to hold many schools of big and little fish and it was supported by a circle of 50 to 65 foot hickory poles pumped deep into the sandy bottom. After the boat was inside the bowl, it would be held against one side while crew members with long gaffs caught the net on the opposite side and slowly pulled the 60 or 70 feet of net in until most of it was in the boat and the trapped fish had been compressed into a small area of very heavy mesh. Then in a usual day they would be mechanically bailed into the boat, the bowl would be fed back into the water, the gate would be dropped and we were homeward bound to our fish house. Having departed at 5:30 or 6:00 A.M., we were often in before noon. Then we'd sort the fish, ice them in barrels and deliver them to truckers for off-Cape markets. One July 4th we made two trips and caught 22,500 pounds of mackerel and five or six giant tuna, all well over 500 pounds.

Tuna were called horse mackerel in those days and they sold for five or six cents a pound. In 1948, according to the *Patriot*, one boat from the village brought in a load of 336 tuna, 300 and 400 pound fish, not the giants that could run 900 pounds or more. It was interesting to see the tuna caught. The bowl would be gradually compressed with the great fish forced to swim in decreasing circles. When one was tired and pressed off balance by the tightened net, two crew members with long gaffs would hook the fish head and tail and bull it to the boat's side for dispatching by a third with a big wooden mallet.

Boatload of tuna caught in 1952. Photo by Adam Rumpkis.
Courtesy of James Ellis who was on the boat. Note long gaffs and wooden mallet.

Being on the water and the fishing increased my love of and respect for the Harbor and the Bay and their bounties that then seemed limitless. However trap fishing out of Barnstable ended by the mid 1950s and the great schools of tuna and mackerel are long gone. Frank Hinckley, a contemporary, told me that one August morning in 1947 he left the Marina at five in the morning as a member of John Vetorino's crew. That day they caught 200 tuna weighing from 45 to 900 pounds; they worked until midnight; and he was paid $5 for the day. It was a hard life.

The business disappeared because it was not profitable. The nets for the leader, heart and bowl were expensive; setting the poles in the spring and removing them in the fall was labor intensive and higher wages were demanded; and the fish stock was fast failing. Although the daily take in the 1940s might include whiting, bone and summer squid, dog fish, a shark from time to time, butter fish, goose fish (then a throw-away, now known as monk fish and considered by some a delicacy), a sea turtle, skate, a few cod, a rare salmon, and once a sturgeon, the principal, saleable fish were mackerel and tuna that came in quantities now gone. In the case of tuna the causes included new fishing techniques, added demand and over exploitation. And so, trap boat fishing, as exciting and as much fun as it was, ended and became a brief chapter in Barnstable's history worth remembering.

Chapter Fifteen

LOST INNOCENTS

What damage have we done to our world? Whales, curlews, clams, tuna and mackerel have all been over-exploited and here are two more instances of questionable good intentions.

Black-crowned night herons, better known by locals as "quawks", and by other less endearing names, were common breeders in large and small colonies throughout Massachusetts. The flock at Sandy Neck bred there at least from 1820, according to Dr. A.O. Gross, an authority on the bird. In 1920 he counted over 2500 nests on the Neck, many in the dunes behind the Little House. The Sandy Neck nests were abandoned in the 1940s, perhaps dynamited as was the case in Brewster. By 1965 there were shifting small colonies in Dennis, Brewster, Monomoy, Chatham, Mashpee, Provincetown, Pocasset and elsewhere; but, the great colony on Sandy Neck was gone and has not returned and the breeding population in the State has dwindled to less than 2000 pairs. What have we lost?

Edward Howe Forbush, the classic nature writer and ornithologist, in his *Birds of Massachusetts and Other New England States* wrote about his July 1908 overnight at the Sandy Neck heron rookery. "As I neared the spot a few herons flapped stiffly away, with hoarse 'quoks'. ...and when at last my load dropped from my weary shoulders...the heronry was so near at hand that the audible cries of both young and old had increased to a steady chorus....Croaks and calls, flat cries and choking gasps filled the air, as the great flocks of the heronry took flight, flapping and wheeling overhead. Here was a beautiful and stirring sight! Hundreds of waving plumes, pale, delicately tinted breasts, great red eyes, and wide-spreading pinions sailing over me just above the trees." When evening fell, he laid out his bedroll and "...lay awake far into the night, listening to the sounds of heronry, marsh and shore. Slowly the dull murk cleared away, then the rosy light melted out of the western sky, the stars came out, but they were soon obscured by dark drifting clouds....for the most part all was still save in the heronry close by. There pandemonium had broken loose - evidently the birds were making a night of it. I had long wished to spend 24 hours at a night heronry, out of curiosity to know whether these birds really turn night into day, as their name implies. ...I never before passed such a night except in some crowded swamps of Florida. No moon was shining, but nevertheless the babel of sounds increased as the night grew darker, until a nervous person might have imagined that the souls of the condemned had been thrown into purgatory, and were bemoaning their fate. One bird in particular in the edge of the wood near me set up a succession of most dismal groans, as if it were suffering slow torture....cat calls, infant screams, shrieks, yells and croaks swelled the chorus, all intermingled with the beating of heavy wings and the harsh 'quoks' of individual birds that swept low over my camping place."

One of my summer nights in the 1960s was spent bass fishing off the Yarmouth flats across from the Point where the channel enters the Harbor. It was lovely and warm and the bass were cooperative on the incoming tide. Finally in the wee hours of the morning I was forced home. All around me that evening the air was punctuated with guttural "quawks" and a croaking chorus of feeding night herons. They were still common then and their calls as they flew over in the morning and evening were part of the wild music we all knew growing up. Old notes remind me that in August of 1972 I chanced upon 27 night herons in the pine woods to the east of the Little House, but to our detriment we have lost a once-common night voice and our world is the poorer because of it.

In the early 1900s seals abounded in the Harbor. They are now rare except for a few winter and spring visitors. One spring we did see over a dozen in front of the Little House sunning on the east end of Great Thatch. One made a great swirl in the calm water alongside my canoe. And once one rose from nowhere in the middle of my decoys: a startling, curious apparition from another world.

Presumably at the behest of fishermen, a seal bounty was instituted. Town Reports from 1890 to 1961 show a bounty per seal of $1 for the first two years, $3 for 1892 through 1934 and $5 for 1934 through 1961. During the whole period bounties were paid for 437 seals. The $3 reward accounted for 230 seals taken from 1890 through 1907 with the largest annual takes in 1893 (25), 1894 (55) and 1895 (40), gradually declining to a single in 1907. The records are silent about seal bounties for 1908 through 1933. After the 26 year silence, a bounty of $5 per seal was paid and 67 seals were killed in the first year, 81 in the second, 25 in the next two and small numbers thereafter through 1961. The $5 bounty accounted for 207 seals.

Harbor seal. Photograph courtesy of Robert Button.

The requisite proof of death at first was an ear, then two ears (to stop an unwarranted run on the Town's Treasury) and finally a nose. Seals congregated in herds on the mid-harbor bar off the Marina. Taisto Ranta recalled several bounty hunters who dynamited the herd, perhaps in 1934-1935 when the total take was 148. Sadly one of them lost a finger and an eye when his dynamite exploded prematurely. There is a story about Shirley Lovell and Parker Holmes spotting a group of seals which had swum up a creek in the Yarmouth marsh. The two men strung a net across the creek mouth and seals, it was said, walked in the streets of Yarmouth.

Needless to say, all this attention did not serve the interests of seal longevity or abundance. In fact, when the government of the Town of Barnstable promised bounty hunters $5 per seal in the 1930s ($5 was a princely sum in those days) the colony of seals that had lived in Barnstable Harbor for many years was doomed. And now, in fact, resident seals are gone: to what avail?

And what comes next? The horseshoe crab we all knew as children is increasingly rare and deserves protection.

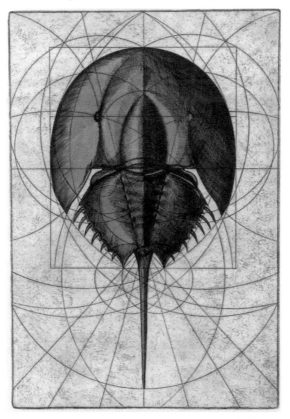

Horseshoe crab print by Charles M. Harden entitled *Remnant*.

When the clam harvests tapered off, seeding was tried. Clam Warden Dottridge blamed the lack of success on horseshoe crabs and in the 1930s looked for and obtained subsidies to eliminate the nuisance. He said the Harbor swarmed with horseshoe crabs. In one day 737 were killed; in one month 3,029. Surprising that the crabs and clams had coexisted in balance for so many centuries. Only when the clam population had been drastically reduced were horseshoe crabs seen as a serious threat to clam propagation. They are harvested now for various reasons and have become much less common than they were 20 years ago. Presumably their eggs, a favored shorebird meal, are more of a rarity too.

It is troubling to think that due to our intervention the curtain may be falling on a creature which has lived on earth for 400 million years.

Chapter Sixteen

GIFTS FROM THE SEA

The tide was unusually low when his rake dragged across something that wasn't clam. The burlap wrapped package contained a more highly prized treasure - jettisoned hooch. While the clammer may have squirreled away some of the prize, word spread quickly and "... a stampede of people... learned of his secret hoard. The serious harvest began on Friday with the low course tide and lasted through Saturday and Sunday when the Coast Guard stepped in to stop the fun. Although it was December, cars appeared from everywhere. One resident said that the 4th of July didn't have more people. A bystander estimated that more than 300 cases of bourbon, rye, champagne, scotch and cognac migrated into local cellars. Boats rigged with pipe drags worked the offshore bars. The drags were three or four foot lengths of pipe with codfish hooks at the ends and a wire bridle attached by a line to the dragging dory. When the Coast Guard came on Saturday afternoon, more than a dozen boats laden with bottles scattered. As each touched the shore a crew member laden down with quarts and pints tucked in his clothes leapt out and disappeared into the laughing crowd. One resident remembered that as fast as the guardsmen filled their truck with confiscated loot and returned to the beach for more, the crowd unloaded it." So reported *The Boston Herald* of December 17, 1933. The job of the Coast Guard was not a popular one.

The 18th amendment was ratified by Nebraska, the 36th state, on January 14, 1919, and prohibition became the law of the land one year later on January 16, 1920. The National Prohibition Act, commonly known as the "Volstead Act", provided for enforcement of the 18th amendment and was passed over President Wilson's veto in October of 1919. Prohibition and what President Hoover called the "noble experiment" lasted until Utah, the last of the 36 required states, ratified the 21st amendment which repealed the 18th and became effective on December 5, 1933. In accepting his nomination in 1932, Franklin Roosevelt announced the 18th amendment was doomed.

Thus began and ended the unique period of 14 years when a federal law affecting much of the adult population was first embraced and then widely disregarded.

In her sermon on January 19, 1920, Reverend Sarah A. Dixon of the Federated Church of Hyannis predicted "If even fairly well enforced it will make the illicit sale of intoxicants a hazardous business, so hazardous that few will be willing to take the risk."

In fact it was during prohibition that cocktails first became popular in the United States.

But it was a dangerous time. The Coast Guard's official history, *Rum War at Sea*, by Malcolm F. Willoughby, from which most of my facts are derived, cites a report that by October of 1930, 200 civilians and 86 prohibition agents had been killed with three times as many related killings at the local level.

In 1921 Captain Bill McCoy carried 1500 cases of illegal hooch into Savannah in his schooner *Henry L. Marshall*. Then he bought another schooner, the *Aretusa*, renamed it the *Tomoka*, and after making arrangements in Nassau, took it with 1500 cases of whiskey to an anchorage off Long Island where the cargo was quickly sold. His supposedly undiluted product became known as the "real McCoy" and he had established the pattern for what became known as Rum Row. He also claimed to have invented the "burlock", six bottles of hooch in a three, two, one pyramid wrapped in straw and burlap for easy and safe handling.

Rum Row eventually is said to have had 100 to 150 vessels, fish boats, schooners, tramp freighters, cargo steamers and yachts, stretched from Florida to Maine carrying 1,000 to 100,000 cases of liquor, anchored at first outside the three mile limit and then outside the so-called 12 mile limit ready to sell to all comers. By the mid 1920s Coast Guard enforcement was at its most effective and the smuggling trade had become largely dominated by criminals.

In late 1924 Coast Guard cutter *Seneca* found the Norwegian steamer *Sagatind* adrift about 40 miles offshore. After a warning shot elicited no response, the *Sagatind* was boarded and the boarding party discovered 43,000 of the original 100,000 cases, $26,000 in cash and a crew stupefied from drink, three with broken jaws, one with a broken leg and many with black eyes. The master said that fights had been a daily occurrence and that he had given up trying to maintain discipline. *Sagatind* was the largest rum runner caught to that date.

Apart from the smuggler's troubles caused by their own cargo and by the Coast Guard, others persisted at Rum Row, particularly piracy. The *Lucille B* of Digby, Nova Scotia, with 1,000 cases was taken off Boston by 15 armed pirates and the crew were forced at gunpoint to load their entire cargo on the hijacker's three boats. The Captain, who had gone ashore, did not return and a double cross was suspected.

Goods from the Rum Row vessels were taken by inshore craft which, after 1924 when the 12 mile limit became effective under international treaty, were increasingly built for high speed and low visibility. Many were powered by World War I Liberty aircraft engines and could travel at 45 knots or faster. These so-called "rum runners" would carry their cargo to local boats or selected locations ashore where often it would be picked up by small trucks and cars and taken over back roads to deserted barns and buildings to await a convenient time for transshipment to its final market. Remote gunning camps were also popular temporary storage facilities. Fishermen were quick to learn that a hold full of liquor was worth more than a hold full of fish. But fish were sometimes used to hide the real cargo. The fisherman's knowledge of local waters and people was valued highly.

When in danger of being caught, the illegal cargo would be jettisoned, reluctantly, often where it could be recovered later. In one reported case, a buoy encased in a salt block tied to the cargo was thrown overboard. When the salt melted the buoy surfaced to mark the treasure. Manila catch lines were sometimes used to facilitate recovery at some more convenient time. The whereabouts of jettisoned hooch often became common knowledge and many small boats carried drag lines just in case. Beachcombing became more popular and on occasion could be highly profitable.

Prohibition generated some interesting numbers. After 1924 the Coast Guard used 25 destroyers to picket the ships on Rum Row with the intent of monitoring off-loading and preventing cargo from reaching shore. At its peak, the Coast Guard's fleet of vessels over 75 feet numbered 330. There was a $30,000,000 committed armada that seized over 1000 vessels engaged in liquor smuggling. Some 649 "blacks", as the rum running vessels were known, were seized and transferred to the Coast Guard and 232 of these were useful in varying degrees. One report estimated that, notwithstanding the massive Coast Guard efforts, 100,000 cases of contraband liquor reached the east coast each month.

In September of 1926, acting on advance information, the police at 3:00 in the morning swooped down on a dozen or more men transferring liquor landed on shore near Barnstable. After a wild scramble, with men running in all directions, the police succeeded in arresting four. Also seized were three trucks, two automobiles, 3,100 gallons of alcohol and 500 quarts of scotch whiskey. A year later a selectman, who was rumored to have been the informant, disappeared, believed by some to have been permanently silenced by the mob.

One Sandwich resident remembered rumbling trucks late at night, groups of men removing some and burying other smuggled liquor along the beach which he and his elders retrieved. Times were hard and he recalled that the hooch, used as currency, was valued at $1 per bottle, a lot of money in those days. Similar stories are told about West Barnstable clammers who also used recovered hooch in trade.

While the Little House may or may not have ever played a role in this ongoing drama, other small gunning camps along the Atlantic coast certainly did. And Barnstable, like most towns on the coast, had its stories. But even today people are reluctant to talk about this bygone, colorful era in our local history.

The old freezer in Yarmouth Port at the mouth of the Harbor is said to have held cargos of liquor. It had a tall stack in which there was a ladder once climbed by one of my contemporaries when he was a boy. Some thought a light would be hung at the top of the chimney to signal rum runners when the coast was clear. Guido Perera, Sr., a highly respected Yarmouth resident and Boston lawyer, early one morning when he was duck hunting saw a converted sub-chaser unloading cases at the abandoned building. Others recall heavy trucks at night rumbling up Keveney Lane, the access road to the freezer.

Invisible from Scudder Lane but near its waterfront to the west was a small boat house, another repository for valuable liquid contraband. A hoard was discovered one day, so I'm told, by Barnstable neighbors who decided to help themselves to the bottled courage. One respected senior citizen parked to watch and, when others went back to get a second load, helped himself to their first. Meanwhile one wife was said to have told her beloved "They're getting hooch at Scudder Lane. You'd better get down there quick before it's all gone."

As the years progressed clam diggers supposedly carried guns while clamming for self protection, but not against saber-toothed clams. When Marcus Howes found hooch on his clam grant he is said to have organized a small party and cleaned out the lot in one night before its discovery became known. The cases sold for around $25 each.

After Prohibition Frank Chase, a long-time Barnstable resident, bought one of the rum running "black" boats from Tiverton, Rhode Island. Before it was repaired, converted to a pleasure craft and renamed *The Wild Knight*, it was powered by three Liberty engines and bullet scarred.

The Wild Knight after its purchase by Frank Chase.
Photo courtesy of Francis Chase.

During the 14 year period of Prohibition customers were never wanting. In 1924 Boston's Club of Odd Volumes met in Barnstable with many of its eminent and renowned members present. The small memorial booklet entitled *The Bake at Barnstable, A Cape Cod Piece*, praises the clams and lobsters and the "…sundry bottles of a non-alcoholic liquid of agreeable taste, as to the provenance of which the Admiral was reticent, not to say evasive. From the labels their domicile of origin appears to have been Scotland."

Running rum was a dangerous game calling heavily on the skills, knowledge and courage of local watermen who worked hard and at risk to slake the public's thirst. Although enforcement efforts were intense, time did not prove Reverend Dixon's prediction accurate. In 1933 the "noble experiment" joined the passing parade and became a hard-to-retrieve part of the Harbor's history.

PART FIVE

Joie de Vivre

"Sport that wrinkled Care derides,
And Laughter holding both his sides . . ."

John Milton *L'Allergro* (1645)

Watercolor of an 18′ Marshall *Sanderling* by Barbara Wylan.

~

Chapter Seventeen

MESSING AROUND IN BOATS

The Barnstable Yacht Club was founded in 1905. It sits about a mile directly across the Harbor from the Little House. There sailboat racing in Barnstable continued after that 1882 race and still does today. Informants tell me that Rainbows (20 footers, plus or minus) were an early racing class and that one survived until 1928. In 1930 or thereabouts three small sailing skiffs built by Cape Cod Shipbuilding were purchased, the *Peanut* by Donald Griffin, the *Zev* by the Wesselhoeft family and the *Bim* by the Coggeshalls. Donald Griffin bought the first Beetle Cat in 1933 and that class is still raced at the Yacht Club. About the same time the Plymouth Yacht Club decided to unload its fleet of Bay Birds and four buyers in Barnstable seized the opportunity for bargain purchases. The Bay Birds were a pretty boat around 18 feet, gaff-rigged with jib and centerboard, but the four purchased had seen better days.

One of the Bay Birds taught me my first lessons about boats and boat ownership. At the end of the summer of 1942 when I was 13 and filled with endless enthusiasm, I bought from a friend the *Sanderling*, the last of the derelict Bay Birds. It was tired but lovely sitting in its barn and the one dollar purchase price seemed reasonable. With friends we managed to drag it on skids over the open road up to an empty barn close to home. The winter was spent in a well-intentioned but generally misguided restoration project. Expert advice was always readily available, how to caulk, paint and pay bills and about other things every owner of a troubled boat should know. For the very bad seams the recommended remedy was caulking, well pounded in, followed by a thick coating of white lead, with a layer of canvas over that, then more white lead with the whole bandage covered by a fitted piece of sheet lead tacked down with copper tacks, three or four to the inch. Summer came and the boat was dragged to the water and anchored to soak and swell. The next morning only the top of the mast showed. We did sail the boat that summer when we weren't bailing. One local wag said it was the only sailboat in the Harbor equipped with running water. Several years later it was sacrificed (so to speak) on the Yacht Club's annual 4th of July bonfire. Perhaps someone watched it burn from the porch of the Little House. I was sleeping off a very long day of commercial fishing, oblivious to the loss of my passing fancy.

During World War II the Beetle fleet dwindled to three boats, but once the war was over interest in competitive sailing bloomed again. Several members of the Yacht Club bought Rhodes 18s, wooden boats manufactured by Cape Cod Shipbuilding. Soon there was an active racing class. Michael Segar's *Snow Goose* was the first fiber glass version and now the original wooden fleet has all been replaced by boats with glass hulls.

The Yacht Club fleet now has expanded to include nine or ten Marshall Sanderlings, 18 foot catboats, which have their own racing series. These shallow draft, roomy boats are well suited to the Harbor and for family outings. Also the young are learning in Optimist Prams and spirited 420s for the more experienced sailors. It's interesting to note that the early Beetles cost about $250 fully rigged; an early Rhodes 18 was bought second hand for $450; and a second hand fiber glass version in 1956 cost $2,000 plus something additional for gentrification. Today a new Beetle fully rigged costs about $17,000 and a Rhodes 18 $13,000. Pleasure boating has become more and more of a luxury.

Harking back to the big old catboats there was one left in the Harbor in the 1940s. She was the *Pelican* owned by Jim Coggeshall who bought her in 1937. She was originally built by Wilton Crosby as a fishing boat for Augustus Eldridge. She measured 22 feet 6 inches and had a three foot bow sprit. Tim Coggeshall, the oldest boy in the family, was 14 when the *Pelican* was bought and he explored in her from 15 on. She was finally sold by the Coggeshalls in 1953. The story has a happy ending for boat lovers. In 2005 the *Pelican* under a new name returned to Barnstable. Tastefully restored, she was approaching her 100th birthday, had been owned by more than 30 people and at the time was owned by John Conway, author of *Cat Boat Summers*. Perhaps he had taken dictation from the old cat, which must have had tales to tell. In 2007 the dowager had her 100th birthday with some of the prior owners attending.

Of course there always was and still is more to life in a boat than racing. There were the long sails with girls, sometimes ending up high and dry in the marshes waiting on the good services of the tide while the no-see-ums took their toll. And there were clambakes and beach parties. The first I remember in the late 1930s ended not quite as planned. We were out of the Harbor just behind the Point when the sun took its usual gentle slide below the horizon. The tide was ebbing and the wind had retired for the evening. The two miles home seemed like 40. Eventually someone's motor boat, and there weren't many in those days, came and towed the five or six Beetles to the Yacht Club. And there were interesting goings on there. Some worried parents were staying at the Barnstable Inn, run at the time by Joe Turpin who according to rumor occasionally took a drink. Joe decided to drive the concerned to the Yacht Club and walked them out to the end dock, by this time high and dry resting on Barnstable's dark-ooze bottom. Joe was in white flannels when he backed off the dock and took his memorable mud bath.

One might well ask about Barnstable as a contemporary port of call. Some sailboat cruising has been done here, but Cape Cod Bay is not at its best as cruising territory. Windless calms are frequent and there are few other anchorages. But some cruising has continued as part of Barnstable's traditions. Consider, for example, happenings in 1938.

In the preceding year a Barnstable boy, Bunny Howard, won the first New England Beetle Cat Championship series held in Barrington, Rhode Island. In 1938 the New England Championships were held on August 1st and 2nd in Barnstable. Six races were scheduled but had to be cut to four because, according to a contemporary newspaper report "...the incoming tide couldn't be hurried to let the racing be started ahead of schedule, and the outgoing tide demonstrated the truth of the old proverb that time and tide wait for no man: and when the tide is about one-third ebb, you just don't race sailboats in Barnstable Harbor." Six crews entered the race representing Angelica Yacht Club of Mattapoisett; Chapaquoit; Bass River; Barnstable; and two Rhode Island towns, Barrington and Edgewood. Each crew drew a lot for the boat to be sailed. At the end of the first day Angelica and Barrington led with Barnstable well behind in third place. On the second day the Barnstable boat took a lead at the start and walked away with the first race. Recognizing that the next race was to be the last, two triangular courses were combined for a long run with both downwind and windward work. Quoting the newspaper again "On the last leg Barnstable and Angelica ran close inshore, so that the first boat to heave in sight of the clubhouse was Barrington, Rhode Island. Jubilation stopped short when both Barnstable and Angelica came in sight around a corner of the boathouse, both nearer the finish line than Barrington. The Barnstable boat finished first and won the Championship. It was captained and crewed respectively by Ned Handy (a cousin of mine) and Tim Coggeshall, both 15 years old.

And what did they do next? Two days later with five contemporaries and three more Beetles they took off on a four day cruise to Provincetown, seven teenagers in search of adventure. Tim Coggeshall kept a contemporaneous log quoted here liberally. They had been planning the trip for a long while. For food each had raided his family's ice box. Bill Wesselhoeft, the oldest boy, was named Commodore and his boat, the *Star*, was the flagship. On the first day they started at 8:00 A.M. in a very light SW wind carried along "mainly by the tide". By the time they were out of the Harbor the wind died completely and two of the boys abandoned their boat and swam around from one boat to another. "There is no danger of having their boat drift away because there is very little current out here. Here's hoping the breeze soon begins to blow again for our destination today is Wellfleet, a port 30 miles from here". At 10:00 still no wind "and we all have had our fill of swimming from one boat to another...None of us are wearing any clothes and the sun is already beginning to show its reddening effects. A poker game is in progress on board the *Star*. The tide will be changing in three hours and unless a breeze comes up by then we shall be carried back towards Barnstable." At 12:00 noon there was still no breeze and they had their "dinner" of sandwiches, cookies and fruit but their chocolate bars had melted in the sun. The boats tied together for lunch and Jim Edwards jumped from boat to boat " making off with the choicest foods of each..." By 2:00 P.M. the wind rose "a honey of a one at that. We are plowing right along." The boats separated slightly and precautions were taken to keep cargo dry by putting it under the deck. "What a beautiful day this is - the water is as blue as can be and there is ne'er a cloud in the sky. The afternoon sun is casting a silver gleam over the water; the west is a carpet that is occasionally broken by the glistening spray of breaking waves." By 4:00 there was a moderately strong SW wind, conditions were choppy with some splash coming on board. "We have been making wonderful time…Hugh and I have played cards a great deal. I am, however, beginning to get sick of that pastime and am looking forward to making camp for the night." By 4:30 they were sailing into Wellfleet Harbor and soon had picked a campsite on a deserted beach. Some of the boys went in to Wellfleet to get drinking water and call home. By 7:00 it was getting dark, all four boats were lying side by side on the beach, calls home had been made and dinner of canned peas, corn and "some kind of meat" was cooking. By 9:30 they had eaten "a fairly decent meal, which, although thoroughly saturated with sand, appeased our hunger." Tim and Hugh washed their utensils as best they could in salt water, stretched the sail over the cockpit and went to bed in their Beetle Cat while the others slept on the beach. They had a kerosene lantern hanging from the boom for light and read themselves to sleep.

The next morning's first entry was at 9:30. It noted that they had slept better than the ones on the beach and that breakfast consisted of sausages, bacon, toast and jam and "some kind of chocolate drink". There was a light fog and departure for Provincetown was delayed until it burned off a bit. By 10:30 they were off the Truro meeting house in large swells that were kindly staying outboard. "…the Beetles ride them beautifully." By 12:30 they were anchored next to a large fishing wharf in Provincetown being watched by curious tourists, "We must have been a queer looking group…tanned, bare-footed and wearing only a pair of waterproof pants. One man asked where we came from and when we replied Barnstable, they were distinctly astounded. Our 12' boats, tiny in reality, must have looked even smaller to the people high on the wharf. When we climbed up onto the wharf, a lot of people asked us questions about our trip, whether we really were from Barnstable and so on. An onlooker would have thought we had sailed around the world instead of 50 or so miles across Cape Cod Bay. By the time we were on shore again, we almost believed we had accomplished a daring feat." Later the boats were beached on Long Point near the Coast Guard station and calls home were made. "Our meat loaf supper would have been cast aside as garbage back home, but it actually tasted good out here...the chocolate drink is getting worse meal by meal, but at least it is something to drink" Two of them took an evening sail in "huge swells" that raised concerns about swamping. Safe and on the way back they saw "...a large beautiful yawl ..." with the same lines as one of the Cup defenders. "We were carrying full sail, but she passed by us as if we were standing still even though she was only carrying a small jib up forward and a reefed jigger aft." That night they all slept comfortably tucked in their bedrolls in their boats.

The next morning the Commodore called for reefs but by 10:00 the boats were beating along the coast toward Wellfleet in heavy swells and light wind. Reefs were shaken out and Tim commented "Not much water comes aboard these little boats - they ride the waves beautifully." The prospect of an all day beat to their destination, East Brewster, was not appealing. "All the fish nets are along here, and it is necessary for us to keep outside of them. A long line of poles through which it is impossible to penetrate stretch from the nets all the way to shore therefore we have to keep tacking outside of them." By noon Tim and Hugh had lunched on crackers, jam, deviled ham and sardines with fruit salad for desert. "What a life! We have both been stretched out on the floor of the boat, steering by the feather on the top of the mast. This would have been disastrous if the wind had shifted but it did not...A thunder storm is backing up against the wind and may catch us." At this point the four boats were spread out over four miles off the Truro shore. By 2:30 they were anchored off a small island in the entrance to Wellfleet Harbor and the thunder storm had passed them by. Soup was warmed over a little sterno stove and it tasted "swell". By 6:30 the boats were together again in East Brewster, two beached, two exploring. Firewood was collected, the boys had a swim and supper of brown bread and beans was ready when the explorers returned. Tim writes "Personally, I think it was the best meal yet, but maybe that is because I cooked the beans! The gnats are out in full force tonight..."

The next morning Tim wrote "The thunder storm hit us finally - not only once but twice. We were awakened at 5:30 by thunder,

Jack Handy and Pete Wesselhoeft and the 12 foot Beetle Cat *Rip.*

and the rain came down. Hugh and I managed to keep inside the boat and dry..." but others had worse luck. The storm let up after a half hour and the boys made one of the other boats a better storm quarters. "When the storm hit again we were fully prepared - four boys in my boat and three in the other. We played cards until the storm stopped. We did not have much of a breakfast - almost all of the food is gone, and anyway we spent most of the time drying out wet clothes etc. in front of the fire...Hugh, Jim, and Pete are engaged slinging mud at one another. P.S. They're in the nude! The breeze is rising steadily, but it's coming from the wrong direction. Again it looks as though we shall have to beat all day." Homeward bound they left the beach, two of the boats far in the lead when disaster struck.

"Of all the luck, the A.D. has been dismasted! Hugh and I were sailing gaily along when suddenly - poof and the mast and sail went overboard." While two boats were out of sight, the third towed them ashore. Both boats were beached in Brewster and the boys found their way first to a phone and then to food. "We decided to use what money we had left in buying some hamburgers and ice cream. The people in the eating place were some shocked to see four tanned salt-covered boys with nothing more than a pair of pants on walk in. We are going to play cards now until Father comes to tow us home."

And come he did in the *Pelican* and towed the two boats home "in the face of a heavy sea". At 7:00 P.M. Tim noted his position "Home!" and that the boys in the lead two boats were spending one more night out, this one on Sandy Neck, perhaps in back of the Little House. "And so ends - the second Beetle Cat cruise. The course was Barnstable to Provincetown on the map, but we touched the Hesperides somewhere along the way!"

Tim Coggeshall grew up to be Barnstable's outstanding sailor. In the winter he taught at Nobles & Greenough, a private boarding school outside of Boston, and in the summers returned to the sea. In 1958 he began taking summer cruises, usually eight each summer and mostly along the Maine coast, with six children on each and one helper. He continued this for 40 summers teaching the joys and challenges of life at sea to over 2000 children. His first boat was a 29 foot 6 inch Winslow cutter named the *Dauntless* and it was replaced by a second *Dauntless*, a 35 foot Sparkman & Stevens sloop rig. Sailing was in Tim's blood and he and his grandsons have enjoyed nights at the Little House probably talking boats. His sailing addiction perhaps harks back to a collateral ancestor, George Coggeshall, a clipper ship captain who retired and wrote *Coggeshall's Voyages*, and to a grandfather who bought a sail boat in Hull, Massachusetts, and sailed it off to Newfoundland - no mean feat then or now.

Over the years other than sailboats have plied the Harbor. The clammers mentioned elsewhere used dories to go to and from the clam beds. In the 1940s and 1950s Henry and Patsy Kittredge still rowed a dory a mile or two up Harbor to Henry's gunning camp on Sandy Neck. In the summer Mrs John Tulis rowed her dory a mile or more from Barnstable to her summer home at the Point. A dory in use today would be a rare sight.

Outboard motors became more common in the 1950s and now there are over 80 motor boats (growing up we called them "stink pots") moored at the Yacht Club compared to 60 regular racing class sailboats. More small sail and motor boats are moored off Scudder's Lane. The marina in Maraspin Creek, greatly expanded in my lifetime, now berths over 175 power boats including many larger pleasure craft and several charter fishing boats. A relatively new mooring field off the mouth of Maraspin Creek has its cluster of big boats. The bigger craft are used primarily outside the Harbor because of the risks of shoal water. This has tended to preserve the Harbor west of the Marina for smaller putt-putts and sailboats. It's interesting to note that in 2005 there were 311 licensed boat moorings in Barnstable Harbor, further moorings in the Harbor are not presently permitted and 276 mooring applicants in 2006 were on the waiting list.

The pleasures of beachcombing are extolled by Henry Kittredge in his book *Mooncussers of Cape Cod* where he does point out that the distinction between beachcombing and wrecking is sometimes fuzzy. Everyone loves a bargain and what could be a better bargain than something found abandoned on the beach. In the old days beachcombers did occasionally became overly enthusiastic and did help themselves to parts of wrecked boats that could hardly be deemed abandoned. This was a more frequent phenomena on the outer arm of the Cape than on Sandy Neck where wrecks were less common. In recent times would anyone strip a boat driven ashore by wind and waves? A report in the January 1975 *National Fisherman* answers the question…at least for 1975.

The 60 foot yacht *Trull* en route from York, Maine, to Old Saybrook, Connecticut, had engine problems and was driven ashore on Sandy Neck by stormy winds and seas. In response to the call for help a Coast Guard vessel came but the grounded boat was beyond help. A helicopter air lifted the two men from their surf washed vessel and carried them to safety. At 9:00 the next morning Taisto Ranta, then Director of Barnstable's Natural Resource Department, learned of the accident and sent two of his officers to the scene. They found the *Trull* high and dry with a group of people, estimated at 40 to 60, stripping the boat. The tools used included axes, crowbars and chain saws. As the tide rose small boats appeared to continue the work. Mr. Ranta told the reporter that he saw the cabin trunk being towed away. When insurance representatives arrived two days after the grounding almost everything was gone. The bow and stern to the waterline had been removed by chain saw. The Natural Resource officers had no authority to stop the looting and the Barnstable police took no action because they had no official notice of the looting, according to the article. The *Trull* was a ten meter racing sloop built in Germany in 1927 and was said to be a classic boat that could never be replaced. The boat's fittings, gear, rigging, instruments, and the rest were reportedly of considerable value. Mr. Ranta had a list of names but charges were not pressed by the owner who hoped instead to recover some of the lifted loot. Ultimately the sea claimed what little was left.

So seafarers take warning, beachcombers in 1975 became wreckers and, although this book is a story of all-embracing change, human nature may be one exception.

To close this chapter on a happier note, competitive sailing in the Harbor is still alive and well. The Little House Log notes a New England Beetle Cat Regatta with strong winds and some capsizing in August of 1986; an Opti Regatta in August of 2001; and an International Rhodes Regatta in August of 2005 with 18 boats competing. For one of the Rhodes racing days there was only a breath of air and we sat on the porch of the Little House watching the boats with their spinnakers, accents of color, barely moving against the tide. On July 24, 2005, the Yacht Club celebrated its 100th birthday with a Parade of Sails. The pomp and ceremony and 32 sailing boats, all splendidly rigged with pennants flying, were watched appreciatively from the Little House and duly noted in the log.

Model of an 18′ Marshall *Sanderling* by Dan Knott.

Chapter Eighteen

A HARBOR DELICACY

To the east of the Little House off Mussel Point there were recently some 20 acres of blue mussels, many above water at low tide and the rest knee-deep or less. Altogether the Harbor had 40 to 60 acres of mussels including extensive beds in deep water to the south of Moon Shoal. These grow faster since they are filter feeders and can feed around the clock. The mussels at Mussel Point, according to Barnstable's shellfish officer, are from a set that got established in 2000 and 2001.The larger ones measure four inches or over, an impressive growth rate for four or five years. Here mussels holdfast to one another or to small stones on the bottom. Those in shallow water are vulnerable to ice flows, our sizeable populations of wintering eider and black duck, as well as their usual predators, spider and green crabs, seagulls, scoter, star fish and, less regularly, people. Somehow quantities survive, living 12 years or more and they are adept at reproducing. A female mussel can release five to twenty five million eggs at a time. They spawn in the spring and at that season lose 25 to 50% of their meat yield. In the last two years our mussel population has sharply declined.

What a spectacular treasure to have at one's doorstep and an extraordinary food source. Note this comparative chart published by the United States Department of Agriculture in *Handbook No. 8, Composition of Foods, December 1963.*

3.5 ounces of raw meat of:	Common blue mussel	T-bone steak (choice)
Calories	95	395
Protein	14.4 grams	14.7 grams
Fat	2.2 grams	37.1 grams
Carbohydrates	3.3 grams	0 grams
Calcium	88 milligrams	8.0 milligrams
Phosphorous	236 milligrams	135 milligrams
Iron	3.4 milligrams	2.2 milligrams
Thiamin	0.16 milligram	0.06 milligram
Riboflavin	0.21 milligram	0.13 milligram

So why for years did Cape Codders and people in New England shun blue mussels?

On November 11, 1620, according to *Mourt's Relation* written the next year, when the Pilgrims reached Provincetown harbor they "...found great mussels, and very fat and full of sea pearls: but we could not eat them: for they made us all sick that did eat, as well sailors as passengers... But they were soon well again." The reaction has been attributed to rich food after long deprivation. Later, when they first reached Plymouth harbor, the same source praises the "Abundance of mussels, the greatest and best that we ever saw." Describing the availability of food, the same text reports "All the winter, we have mussels...". Thomas Morton in *New English Canaan* writes "Mussels there are infinite store, I have often gone to Wassaguscus: where were excellent mussels to eat (for variety) the fish is so fat and large." So mussels were appreciated in the early years by Pilgrims and also by Indians as shown by their shell middens on the Neck. Popular for centuries on the continent, perhaps they were less so in England. The fact remains that for years they were not popular in New England. Mrs. D.A. Lincoln founder and superintendent of the Boston Cooking School wrote *The Boston Cook Book* in 1884. It was the only cookbook included in the 1946 Grolier Club exhibition entitled *One Hundred Influential American Books Printed Before 1900*. My copy, with a preface dated 1894, has 12 pages of shellfish recipes, including one under the heading *Reptiles* (for frogs) but not a word about mussels.

Fannie Farmer, a student of Mrs. Lincoln's and her successor as principal of the Boston Cooking School, wrote her enormously popular *Boston Cooking School Cook Book* in 1896. Our 1930 edition has 17 pages of shellfish recipes with no mention of mussels. An earlier edition says only that mussels were eaten in England and Europe and were like oysters but of inferior quality. And mussel recipes are equally absent from the pages devoted to shellfish in the little cookbook written in 1911 by my grandmother, Amy L. Handy, titled *What We Cook On Cape Cod*.

In 1896 Oscar Tschirky wrote *The Cookbook of "Oscar" of the Waldorf* and there finally we do find seven mussel recipes but Oscar was not cooking for Cape Codders. So we are left with the question of why for so many years New Englanders did not eat blue mussels, so delicious and prized today here and overseas.

According to various internet sources, the contemporary blue mussel industry in the United States generates $10,000,000 annually. In 2000 we consumed 27,000 metric tons compared to 200,000 metric tons consumed in Spain. Many of our mussels are imported from Chile, China and Canada although more and more are being farmed in the United States. Wild mussels, particularly ours from the Harbor, taste better, according to our son, Jeb, who is in the seafood business and has a keen sense of taste.

There was a limited market for mussels here before it began to bloom after the Second World War. Travelers returning from Europe were hungry for more of the mussels they had relished in France steamed in wine with shallots or served in Italy with pasta and a variety of sauces or in Spain in casseroles like paella or in Belgium where street venders sold them as French fries.

One Barnstable boy in the 1950s helped put himself through Yale and medical school selling mussels he harvested off Mussel Point. At that time there was demand in New York if not locally.

And now many of us have discovered the delights of the bountiful crop. Recreational permits allow a bushel a day any day of the week and shellfish personnel have even taken groups out to encourage the harvest. Before the crop dwindled, we could run out from the Little House or from the Barnstable shore in a small motorboat and wading fill a peck basket with mussels in less than half an hour. With the spoils come seaweed, mud, crabs, starfish and other small wildlife of interest to little people. The real project starts at home where we scrub, remove the barnacles, pull the beard (the byssus threads, the mussel's holdfast), wash off the mud and complete preparation for cooking. It can be a pleasant pastime for a summer's afternoon. After the mussels are well cleaned and scrubbed, here are four of our favorite recipes.

Steamed
Three quarts of cleaned mussels in their shells
One half cup of dry white wine
Two cloves of garlic
Two tablespoons of olive oil
Melted butter

Steam mussels in the wine, garlic and olive oil until they open. Serve in large bowl with melted butter as a dip. Serves six as a first course.

Mussels Linguine

Three quarts of cleaned mussels in their shells
One half cup of water
One half stick of butter
One half cup of olive oil
Four cloves of garlic chopped
Three quarters cup parsley chopped
Package of linguine
Parmesan cheese

Steam mussels until they open. Reserve a quarter cup of clean mussel broth. Remove mussels from shell and chop. Saute garlic in oil and butter. Add mussels, the mussel broth and parsley and serve on freshly cooked linguine topped with Parmesan cheese.

Billi Bi Soup

Created at Maxim's in Paris for William B. Leeds, a wealthy American businessman who ate there often in the 1920s, the cold mussel soup became a French favorite.

This recipe is from *The American Heritage Book of Fish Cookery* by Alice W. Houston and is included here with the permission of American Heritage Publishing Co., Inc.

> 1 pound mussels
> 2 tablespoons chopped fresh parsley
> 3 tablespoons butter
> Salt and freshly ground pepper to taste
> 1 medium onion, chopped
> 2 cloves garlic, chopped
> 1 cup heavy cream
> 1 cup dry white wine

Scrub mussels well.

In a frying pan, heat butter, add onion and garlic and saute until onion just begins to soften.

Add mussels and wine. Cover closely and cook until shells open, about 5 to 10 minutes.

Remove mussels and set aside.

To the broth, add parsley and season with salt and pepper. Stir in cream and reheat very briefly. Serve in bowls garnished with mussels.

Yield: 4 servings

A beaten egg yolk can be added before the final heating. We enjoy Billi Bi hot or cold.

Janet's Famous Recipe

Here is an enthusiastic endorsement of local mussels from the log dated September 1991

> After scooping some mussels from Mussel Point Janet steamed them in her now famous garlic/tomato broth. Followed by succulent swordfish we remained in a food coma for some time.

And here is the famous recipe in Janet's own words:

> "In a large pot saute in olive oil: 4 minced garlic cloves; 1 diced onion; diced celery; chopped parsley; add a bit of white wine; salt and pepper. Pick or purchase 10 or so really perfect tomatoes. Dip tomatoes in boiling water and peel off skins. Add peeled tomatoes.
> This makes a light tomato broth.
>
> Take this pot out to Sandy Neck with you by boat. On the way, collect mussels from the best spot you can find. Deep water mussels that have never been exposed are best. Throw out the anchor and use the forks of the anchor to haul in huge clumps of mussels.
> Clean mussels.
> On a Coleman stove overlooking Barnstable Harbor heat up your pot of fragrant broth to a simmer and add the mussels. Close the lid. Mussels will open....
>
> Enjoy this on the front porch of the Handy's cottage. Perfection."

Janet has moved away but still has a warm spot for Barnstable and its mussels.

Chapter Nineteen

OTHER VISITS

The Little House became a pleasure trove. Share here with visitors their fun, warmth and enthusiasm.

Each visit starts with a trip to sea, a short one but for land animals a radical change from ordinary life.

In the beginning we traveled by canoes which treated us kindly in good weather. On those trips we were Indians delighted by the paddle's surge and the bubbling hiss as we slid through the quiet water. If the wind came up, however, the walk home was long.

Then we graduated to the smack of canvas and the glories of sail. And sailing out has always been best. In Barnstable the vessel of choice was and is a small, shallow-draft boat with a center board. We started with a 12 foot Beetle Cat, moved to a 14 foot Handy Cat, the *Bay Bird*, and then to an 18 foot Marshall Sanderling, the *Old Squaw*. One log entry refers to "going to sea in ships", a somewhat exaggerated vision of grandeur.

Sailing adventures at night were always stimulating…

> Last evening we took off for the house at high tide
> (about 10:30 PM) & sailed, on a reach, toward the
> Town beach. Hit Green Point which I worked
> us off, then went aground again near Braley's.
> Sue was the skipper with the tiller & view. Finally
> got in - centerboard lost its wooden block, Sue
> lost the anchor line, I slipped in a pot hole, Sue
> knocked new flashlight into water (it stopped but
> is working this morning) & we had a lovely time.

Another evening, described in Sue's words:

> The five oldsters sailed home in shrouded moonlight
> & slight drizzle singing Cole Porter songs & going
> aground on Little Thatch just once.

Testifying to the ingenuity and restlessness of man, new modes of transportation were tried from time to time. More in scale with our operation was the sailfish which on one high tide we towed across our marsh frontage in knee deep water and tied to the steps of the Little House. Then came the windsurfers, fine high-steppers at times, at others unruly.

> Still stiff from yesterday's windsurfing- too
> much chop. I never got to the Neck but had
> lots of practice getting on and off the board.

Thinking back, getting off didn't take much practice.

A fine newcomer here and perfectly suited to Barnstable is the kayak, first mentioned in the log on September 18, 1989. Interesting that we find ourselves reverting to Indian canoes and Eskimo kayaks and find both so elegant and satisfactory for pursuing today's pleasures on Cape Cod. Now it's rare if some of our guests don't come by kayak.

Acknowledging the important ceremonial aspect of sailing, the Little House deserves, and here shall have, recognition as the site of the organizational meeting of the *Barnstable Fat Cat Association*. The meeting took place August 19, 2001, on the porch and included most Barnstable owners of 18 foot Marshall cats. There was a fine lunch and the *Association* has been in hibernation ever since.

Before leaving the nautical phase of a visit to the Little House, truth requires admission that our amphibious operations have always been supported by a 14 foot motor boat.

After the anchor is thrown comes the "All Ashore" call followed by "Don't forget the children, keys and gear!" Guests scramble up the marsh bank and stop to look. There to their front are the miles of flat marsh meadow flanked by inviting dunes; to their left the twinkling sea; and directly ahead and close the weathered, gray gunning shack standing alone silhouetted against the brilliant white sand.

First visitors often wax eloquent. Here are some favorite first impressions

> A friend brought us to see the shack...What a memorable
> place...a place to remember like an old friend. (Unknown).

> First visit here on the world's most perfect evening.
> Trudging onto the dunes was magical - watching the
> Harbor change with the tide was poetic.
> (Barnstable painter).

Tropical weather -beautiful sunset - healthy poison ivy-
great rocking chairs - ready to retire here (Brown professor).

The most beautiful home a person could have.
(A young Barnstable woman prone to overstatement).

Our first visit...What a wonderful piece of heaven -
the cottage by the sea. A day to remember; a trek to
the water, a kayak trip here, lunch on the porch and
lots of great memories we won't forget for a long time.
(A friend of Jeb's).

Some first visits did less for the muse but were just as noteworthy.

The Chace's were eaten by large voracious bugs.
Sandy Neck is bug heaven! Postscript : mosquitoes
worst ever - like Arctic tundra - hundreds on our
legs at dusk when we arrived -none on porch so we
stayed, nibbled, imbibed & spent a lovely hour. At
departure, Liz in a filmy, white pant suit did an otter
slide down the mud bank and SPLASH. Kim said he
was having a wonderful time as we splashed home
through the rough, cold waves. Very memorable
with lots of laughs.

Many friends have come, seen and been conquered by the
charms of the Little House. If their testimonials are to be
believed (and like yours, our friends are noted for outstanding
wit, intelligence and honesty), they have taken away special
memories to treasure. One brief entry describes coming back
after a too long absence as

An old lover's tryst.
And others join the chorus.

My first time out here in two years? I missed it and
thought of the Neck often - the dunes, swimming at
the back beach and in the marshes, beach plums, clams
and blueberries.

This is truly one of the most beautiful places on earth,
especially on a gorgeous July evening after a cool and
cloudy day.

. . . pure heaven to be out in this perfect spot again on a
lovely morning, little wind, timeless beauty.

Inevitably there are special visits to remember and treasure. Ann and Malcolm Kerr porch sat with us in 1982 before they moved to the Middle East, he to take over as president of the American University of Beruit. It was a rushed visit but Ann did find time for a quick painting. We celebrated her 50th birthday in 1984, after Malcolm's assassination. Her entry...

> Oh to be able to turn the clock back to my last entry...
> Now I am sitting here on your porch contemplating
> new beginnings & the beauty of sea & sky & birds
> which seem to go on forever.

Very early on one Saturday evening we brought Gordon Marshall and Louise Austin out to inspect the sunset. Gordon was a prior owner of the Little House along with Louise's deceased husband. Louise then was in her late 80s, lively and entertaining company but not able to negotiate the path into the house. I remember how light she was to carry over our mosquito-ditch bridge. We had a fine visit. Both now have departed for other places we hope as beautiful.

Another time friends from Washington hiked down from Henry Kittredge's cottage, the Barnacle, on the Point. Their walking time was 25 minutes. Recognizing the rare opportunity, we tried but failed to solve any of the concerns caused by people within the Beltway. This visit was a highlight because residents of the Neck tend to be engrossed in their own projects with little time for gadding about.

Ned and a painter friend, John Hagen, canoed out on Oct. 30, 1984.

> Went deer stalking... got stumped. Lots of tracks
> Walked through woods to back beach, one Jeep. John
> did rough sketch for masterpiece.

John added "Breathtaking afternoon" The painting that resulted from this visit, reproduced on the title page to Part Three, is one of our favorites.

For children it is an exciting wonderland of rough-and-tumble adventure and discovery. Their usual first reaction is to the vast sandbox. Our Grandchild, Alex, referred to the dunes as "sand mountains"; his younger sister to the "huge doons". When seven Alex wrote (with the letter "y" reversed)

SANEy NECK is my FANTASE

115

Alex: "doon" hopping.

An old photograph dating from the turn of the last century shows a well-dressed little urchin clambering up a dune presumably to roll down. We did it and the sand stayed with us it seemed forever. The log has children's notes that refer to dune rolling; "a hill hopping walk to the Indian doons"; walking in the "scorching hot sand"; kids playing Frisbee golf and "dunorama". Frisbee golf caught on even with the adults. It involved laying out a number of target "holes" for each player to approach with Frisbee throws, the lowest number winning the hole. Even in the chilly evenings on the Neck, Frisbee golf could generate a fair amount of heat. The rules for dunorama never found their way into the history book so it must be viewed a "lost" amusement.

Sam, another grandchild, when he had just turned 11, wrote:

We spent the night in the house, then went to look for taily-po prints. Spooky

And his companion from an inner city school had this to say about the same visit:

First we got in a speed boat and went to sandy neck to the cabin then we talked a little then we went in the marshes

116

> and I sunk then we went to an Indian shell heap then at
> night we played cards then we wresled with ned then
> we laid down and talked starwars and tailypo then
> we went to sleep then we woke up and watched the
> sun rise and then we went to look for tailypo prints

Another boy from the same school summarized his experience...
> It was the worst and the best thing in the world.
> The worst part was when we went to the mud.
> Astin got mud all over himself. Then
> we had a mud fight that was the Best part

To young visitors this place of dunes, marsh, stunted pines, isolation and crude shelter is an awesome paradise.
> At about nine o'clock in the night we saw three
> gigantic thunder storms come through the bay. Heavy
> thunder and huge bolts came every few seconds!!!!!!
> It was ...awesome
> well we survived it and have had breakfast, after
> exploring in our pajamas.

This is a young Elizabeth Nill.
> Although it was buggy, I had a great time sleeping
> on the porch! We were looking up and saw a shooting star
> fly across the sky! It was really exciting.

For children night brings hobgoblins even in their own secure bedrooms back home. Night comes closer and is more of a presence on Sandy Neck. One night in the cabin, when long shadows were thrown by flickering fire light, Calvin, a college friend, read the *Speckled Band*. His big voice and sense of drama brought Sherlock Holmes to Sandy Neck and young and old alike listened apprehensively for footsteps on the porch and the sounds of things that slither in the night.

Spooky at times, maybe so, but what a wonderful place to be uninhibited. When night falls kerplop the log memorializes small ones "noisely playing pig" and older ones, after a beer or two, playing...
> cards like riverboat gamblers and there seemed
> to be at least a kernel of truth in most of the stories told.

117

And what a splendid time to make music, with a soft and sweet guitar, or sometimes with all available noise makers. Here the old folks are entertaining Alex, age four…

> Idled away an hour making music with Alex, the recorder and miscellaneous percussion pieces (triangular file, screw driver, big spike and oar lock). We are good!
> John and I sang and played; Alex played and danced. House flies joined the fun. There's a Laughing Gull here. I wonder why.

Children add an important dimension, not only to all life, but particularly to life on Sandy Neck. It has been a joy watching them grow and treasure their childhood enthusiasms and memories. One year Elizabeth Nill wrote. . .

> A few tips on peeper toad hunting: be quick and gentle….Every time we come it gets more and more special.

Edie Vonnegut Squibb had this to add . . .

> Wanted to recreate for my kids what my parents did for me when I was a kid, which is the incredibly delicious memory of picnics on Sandy Neck, with perfectly warm night and delicious food and running in the dunes and brilliant sunset. FOOD for their memory banks.

This magic spot has certainly helped with parent-child bonding. Ned and Polly and their two young boys

> Had a memorable dinner together filled with laughter… After dessert we lay down in the dunes to watch shooting stars and talk about the universe.

And here is Ned reporting on a visit with the two boys alone.

> The house has provided outdoor excitement and much needed freedom to two boys in need of both. We had a long walk in the woods, some marsh stomping, a great burger dinner, some discussion, a beautiful sunset, beautiful sunrise, a walk to the back beach and most importantly some loud, long laughs!

Our children have cherished the privilege of being alone with their children sharing the solitude and timeless beauty of Sandy Neck.

Meanwhile the elders have invented their own entertainment, in addition to tippling and admiring sunsets. Ned and Polly canoed out one evening and . . .

were enthusiastically greeted by the million mite march. Fixed a couple of dark and stormys and headed for the "back seven". Polly prevailed on 3 out of four holes, but the midges were the real winners.

That's how golf came to Sandy Neck.

Built as a gunning camp, we did try at various times to put it to its intended use. On October 13, 1979, son Jeb, then almost 20, and I

...did our first shooting together-lots of shooting. We came by canoe at about 5:30 AM - too early, much too early. Dawn coincided with rain & high tide. We shot the shore with no cover & no shots but lots of sightings. A Kingfisher almost landed on our heads but left abruptly in a flurry of wing beats and irate exclamations. Then we went to Great Thatch...more sightings and rain. Then to the east point of Little Thatch where the cover was good and the shooting excellent. We pulled in 8 or 10 blacks and pulled out with none, having used our shells. Back to house, wet through & hoping Sue would come. We had a fire, coffee & just as the tide seemed too low our dog Chamois appeared on the marsh bank, followed by Sue & Seth with sustenance. We all had a cheerful and long lunch by fire light, listening to the rain & drying clothes. Now about 2:30 & Jeb & I will be off again in about a half hour. Windy, still raining but not cold. No other hunters in the immediate area & surprising numbers of birds. Season opened on the 10th - the birds are novices like us. This is my first time in over 10 years. All snoozing now and all's well with the world -if wet.

Later that afternoon Jeb wrote this terse addendum

We had second thoughts because of rain. Had a great time snoozing in front of the fire.

Subsequent notes report takes of blacks, eider and mergansers but we never posed much of a threat to the duck population. Here is the last hunting note worth repeating

> Jeb and I are shooting-after a fashion. ...We had one long shot & scared the bird; some, not much. Tide's nearing high & wind's thumping against the shutters. Have a nice fire & gray chill, a guest slow to leave.... Seal, quite light colored, paid our decoys a quick visit. There are Eider, some Brant & a flight of geese went over us - just too high for a shot, but magnificent.... Jeb's off for a jump shot & I'm going out to watch & cheer for the duck!

Gradually the Little House evolved into something more than a place for gunners to drink, sleep and get warm.

After a long walk, a brisk swim and breathing the fresh and tangy salt air, what could be better than a good meal! And many have been provided at the Little House. Breakfast for seven, for example

> ...a dozen eggs, ham, coffee, orange juice, English muffins done on the new toaster (it's slow and burning up - Frank says " Sacrificing itself to save the muffins") & home grown honey.

For lunch, always with a cold, crisp white wine, cherry stones on the half shell, or

> ...blue fish, chicken, basil & parsley blowing in the wind

or home baked bread and

> brie, fruit, yogurt and brownies

Cruising once in a fancy yacht out of Hadley's Harbor, we passed at close quarters a strong-smelling fishing boat, homeward bound and showing hard use. Memorable when the grizzled skipper called up "Any Grey Poupon?" The Little House might be short on elegance, but not the meals!

In the evenings the usual sunset drinks are followed by a variety of main courses with hamburgers, charcoal broiled, being the children's favorite. Steamed clams are a fine addition or substitution. One note recalls

> ...a superb cocktail hour and sensational dinner of broiled bluefish (aluminum foil shiny side in), fresh peas and left over casseroles as good as ever.

120

Lobsters boiled in salt water are delicious and one visitor's note refers to two big ones brought from his own traps in the Harbor. Steak is popular. One friend considers it dangerous; others are less cautious.

> We had a swim last evening, steak and some of our plentiful and magnificent garden tomatoes, Argentine wine, a fire, etc. Lovely evening with a blustery wind, a clearing cold front and a sky wiped clean flecked with stars with a bright glow from a waning moon.

Another evening

> Sat over martinis & lovely sunset. Supped on fresh garden green beans, potatoes cooked at home & steak & cukes, tomatoes, basil, parsley, etc. from garden . . . toasted marshmallows.

One happy camper reported

> A great meal was topped off by a gourmet dessert: marshmallows roasted over candles and then stuffed in between an Oreo. Yummy!

One chilly anniversary we had fillet cooked in the fireplace, asparagus, couscous and champagne. It was a rare pleasure to eat by firelight and be entertained by long shadows dancing on the rustic walls.

For several years the boys went to the Centerville River and caught blue crabs. Their technique was to wade barefoot in the mud and, with luck, scoop up the crabs with a long-handled net. Blue crabs are fast, testy and have noteworthy pincers. The high sport was who got whom first, boy or crab. A mid-August entry noted that crabs were running and that the

> <u>Cape Cod Crab Club</u> met and ate dozens of crabs
> ... a great feast

May there be many more as enjoyable.

What about the isolation and solitude? One day our children walked half way to the Point and paid a call on an elderly woman who lived all alone in a very isolated house.

> Met 77 year-old Ms. Fogerty. We told her about a gov't car parked down the road and she
> said "You can't be a worry-wart and live on Sandy Neck ." She has been coming here since 1925...

The peace and quiet are bliss for our married children.

AAAAHHHHH - That is a sigh of deep contentment. We sat on the porch and talked - What a luxury. We read, I napped, Ned walked. We had an early dinner of tuna, wild rice salad and tomatoes & mozzarella. We fished right off the house and caught a couple of small stripers...We watched as a smoldering sun eased itself below the horizon and a luminous almost full moon assumed the challenge of lighting our way home. ...Thank you Sandy Neck for a chance to recharge our souls.

There is peace on Sandy Neck and goodwill to men.

Peace reigns here - if not elsewhere.

But friends and family do gather at the getaway.

122

Chapter Twenty

MORE DELICACIES

Lobsters

Consider first the lobster. Drawing on his experiences with the Plymouth colony, Thomas Morton in *New English Canaan* wrote [the spelling is contemporary]:

"Lobsters are there infinite in store in all parts of the land, and very excellent. The most use that I made of them, in 5 years after I came there was but to bait my hook for to catch bass, I had been so cloyed with them the first day I went ashore.

This being known, they shall pass for a commodity to the inhabitants; for the savages will meet 500, or 1000, at a place where lobsters come in with the tide, to eat, and to save dried for store, abiding in that place, feasting and sporting a month or 6 weeks together."

And we know Governor Winslow found Indians foraging for lobsters in Barnstable Harbor when he came in 1621 looking for the lost John Billington.

Skipping a few hundred years, we find a Barnstable Harbor House handbill which offers "... clam chowder, clambakes, and lobster furnished for parties at short notice. Fruit, confections, peanuts & etc. constantly on hand and for sale cheap. Ginger ale, birch, lemon and vanilla soda- Cigars and tobacco. Seafowl shooting months of October & November." The Harbor House was the eatery next to the lighthouse on the Point that was run in the 1890s by Benjamin Lovell and his son Herbert. The lobsters were probably brought in by the Lovells from nearby pots. Shirley Lovell, of the next generation and his son, Herbert, both trapped lobsters in Cape Cod Bay as a life profession.

Even today there are a few caught in the Harbor but lobsters now are never infinite in supply as Winslow said they were "in their time". Quite the opposite, they are rare all the time.

Oysters

Morton enthuses over New England's oysters. "There are great store of oysters in the entrance of all rivers; they are not round as those of England, but excellent fat, and all good. I have seen an oyster bank a mile at length."

When Taisto Ranta excavated the remains of the Indian maiden on Sandy Neck he noted that oyster shells were heavily predominant in the midden along with scallops and then clams and some quahogs.

There are no "wild" oysters in the Harbor now except for a set maintained by the Town at the foot of Scudder Lane for recreational harvest. This resource has been popular and has had its ups and downs due primarily to predation. The recreational harvests in 2000 and 2006 were, respectively, 500 and 200 bushels. The Town figures 200 oysters per bushel so at 50 cents apiece the 200 bushels would have a value of $20,000. Farmed oysters, on the other hand, are doing well and are being grown and sold in increasing quantities. The reported harvest for 2003 was about 500,000 pieces with an estimated market value of $250,000.

Quahogs

First a note about spelling: "quahog" is the more common spelling today but "quahaug" is also acceptable. Throughout the book, the shorter spelling is used except where the longer version is used in a quote.

David Belding, M.D. was Biologist for the Commonwealth of Massachusetts in the first decade of the 1900s. As such he wrote several tracts, one titled *The Quahaug Fishery of Massachusetts* and designated *Marine Fishery Series-No. 2*. Most of my facts about quahogs derive from Dr. Belding's learned work. Among others he describes this method of harvest:

"*Treading*: The early settlers in Massachusetts quickly learned from the Indians the primitive method of 'treading' quahaugs, which required no implements except the hands and feet. The 'treader' catches the quahaug by wading about in the water, feeling for them with his toes in the soft mud, and then picking them up by hand. Nowhere in Massachusetts is it now used as a method of commercial fishery."

Without help from the Indians, my children learned to "tread" quahogs in the soft mud by the Little House and on the nearby islands. If one can avoid or tolerate the no-see-ums, treading is one of the world's special primitive pleasures.

A sad story in Bradford's history seems to relate to treading. For various reasons Thomas Weston with several others left the Plymouth Colony and moved north along the coast to establish their own settlement. Bradford writes that they squandered their own stores and mistreated the Indians so "In ye end, they came to that misery, that some starved & dyed with could & hunger. One in gathering shell-fish was so weake as he stuck fast in ye mudd, and was found dead in ye place." As far as I know, all quahog treaders in Barnstable have escaped this risk.

Locally at least we try not to refer to quahogs as clams, a designation reserved for our soft-shells. Quahogs 1 1/2 to 2 1/4 inches are "little necks" and from there to 3 inches are "cherry stones". Bigger ones have no common name and are generally set aside for chowder, baking or clam pie. A 2 inch quahog may be 2 1/2 years old and 3 inch individual a year older. Belding referred to quahogs as a southern species and suggests that the north side of the Cape approaches the northern limit of their range. He specifically says they are found only in "isolated patches" in Barnstable Harbor and adds "...at present the total area of quahauging grounds is hardly 5 acres." It may be they are not available in commercial quantities, but digging quahogs is a favorite sport, summer and winter, and the permitted peck is the usual reward. As to methods of harvest, treading is reserved for summer in the warm water and mud; a basket rake is useful winter and summer in deeper water; and a long-handled rake with five or six fine tines is best above low water. All family members (if they can be borrowed from other projects) can help considerably with the harvesting.

An organization, known as The Barnstable Association of Recreational Shellfishermen, or BARS for short, meets regularly, includes about 175 members and watches over the interests of recreational shellfishermen.

Taisto Ranta believes the farmed quahogs have increased the quantity in the Harbor available for recreational digging. That's not surprising based on Dr. Belden's spawning facts: the average number of eggs for a 2 1/2 inch quahog is about two million; and an acre of shore with an averagely dense population of 2 1/2 inch cherry stones may throw out "…800 billions of eggs." There are approximately 90 acres of farmed quahogs in the Harbor and many of the eggs must drift free, some to establish new beds. In 2003 farmed quahogs from the Harbor were reported at over 3,043,943 pieces with a market value of over $600,000.

While family and friends enjoy little necks and cherry stones, with a good accompaniment of chili sauce, horse radish and lemon, we also like the bigger ones baked. This is a recipe we have found particularly good from *The American Heritage Book of Fish Cookery* by Alice W. Houston. The recipe is published with the permission of American Heritage Publishing Co., Inc.

Stuffed Clams

1 dozen cherrystone clams	2 tablespoons butter, melted
4 tablespoons olive oil	Salt & freshly ground pepper,
1 medium onion, chopped	to taste
2 cloves garlic, minced	1/4 teaspoon oregano
1 tablespoon chopped fresh	1/4 cup grated Parmesan cheese
parsley or chives	Lemon juice
1/2 cup fine bread crumbs	

1. Preheat oven to 400 degrees F.
2. Shuck clams, chop and set aside. Reserve half the shells, wash well, and set aside.
3. In a frying pan, heat olive oil. Add onion, garlic, and parsley (or chives), and saute until just soft. Off the heat, add clams and toss lightly.
4. Combine bread crumbs, butter, salt, pepper, and oregano.
5. Grease each clam shell. Divide clam mixture evenly among shells. Top each shell with crumb mixture. Sprinkle with Parmesan and a squeeze of lemon juice.
6. Place on baking pan and bake in a 400 degree F. oven for 10 minutes, or until crumbs are browned. Yields six servings.

And here is the official clam chowder recipe of BARS. It is outstanding!

BARS Chowder

1/2 pound of butter	7 medium Spanish onions diced
3 bay leaves	10 medium potatoes cubed
2 quarts of quahog broth	2 quarts of quahog meat chopped

Cream or half and half for consistency
Salt & white pepper to taste

1. Melt butter, add onions and cook until transparent.
2. Add bay leaves and diced potatoes. Mix until well coated with butter and onions.
3. Add broth and bring to a boil.
4. Cook until the potatoes are tender and remove from heat.
5. Add chopped quahogs and stir well. Salt and pepper, add cream to the consistency you want.

Scallops

Scallops in the Harbor are something of a mystery. The shells are found in the Sandy Neck middens and Taisto speaks of a large pile of scallop shells that existed years ago at the end of Bone Hill Road at the east end of the Harbor. Dr. Belding in the early decades of the 1900s wrote *The Scallop Fishery of Massachusetts, Marine Fisheries Series - No. 3* which among other things reports that scallops live only two years, that they do not migrate or swim long distances and that Barnstable Harbor did not have enough "… to support a regular business." He warns that first year scallops cannot be harvested without reducing the breeding stock. Scallops were once thought to be poison and became of commercial importance only after the 1870s. A bushel of scallops in the shell yields on the average 2 1/2 to 3 quarts of "eyes", the edible adductor muscle. Today bay scallops are considered one of the world's finest marine delicacies and are priced accordingly.

There were scallops in Barnstable but the quantities diminished in the 1950s. They became more plentiful in the fall and were regularly harvested with a dip net off Scudder Lane. Then in 1969 there was a scallop bonanza on the Indian Trail and Bone Hill

Road flats at the east end of the Harbor. The weather was mild in the early fall when the season opened and on the weekends the exposed flats were dotted with crowds of men and women, old and young, in colorful garb harvesting the marooned scallops often by hand. That fall over 17,000 bushels were taken from the Harbor. Since then pickings have been slim to non-existent.

On November 22, 1953, Francis ("Frank") Taylor, a 60 year-old, went on an early-morning scalloping expedition off Bone Hill Road with his friend, Charles W. ("Chuggie") Jones. Both were long-time Barnstable residents and had spent many days together on the same flats. But this day was different and a heavy fog shrouded the extensive bars and disoriented the two. Chuggie, the taller, not swept off his feet by the incoming tide, was saved. Frank was less fortunate and his body, notwithstanding intensive searches by firemen, police, volunteers, and the Coast Guard, was found sometime after the November 25th *Patriot* that first reported the loss went to press.

Fog in the Harbor, like cold, deserves special respect, particularly because it is an infrequent phenomenon.

Razor Clams

Razor clams, difficult to dig and said to be as sweet as bay scallops, are still harvested. Recent commercial takes have been around 3,000 bushels.

Our generous Harbor continues to provide a living for commercial diggers and growers and multiple pleasures for recreational hunter/gatherers and their families.

Chapter Twenty One

FISH STORIES

The time has come for a few Harbor fish stories. First, an observation: fish have their appeal but it is the monomaniacal fishermen who deserve closest attention. The Harbor has generated lots of these. A tribute here must be paid to Barnstable's premier fisherman, George "Red Dog" Warren. Some people live for wine, women and song, some for money, some for golf, some to impress their neighbors. George lived for fish and fishing.

It was a splendid moonlight night in 1954 when we first met George. Sue and I had canoed out and were fishing off the flats at the end of Indian Trail. She was large with child, waist deep in the incoming tide and bathed in moonlight. Big, blonde and beautiful she must have looked like some Nordic goddess, at least George thought so when he first emerged from somewhere and fixed his gaze on this statuesque earth mother. I was very much an incidental part of the story as George retold it many times. The idle conversation and fishing talk led to an invitation to join George the next day on his boat, the *Fish Hawk*. Later we learned that it was the prized possession of George and two other passionate fishermen/school teachers. As best I recall, our first trip on the *Fish Hawk* was unproductive as far as the fishing went but we certainly caught a wonderful and unique friend.

George was all fisherman and a beacon for our children growing up. A bundle of contradictions, the two constants in his world were a love of fishing and a strong distaste for Republicans who he tended to blame for everything that went wrong, including bad weather. He had grown up in Greenwich, gone to Andover and Yale with George Bush and by the time he was in his mid-fifties retired on inherited money; but, like socialists of times gone by, he felt wealthy people in general and Republicans in particular were the bane of our society. He liked salmon fishing and going to Harbor Island in the Bahamas for bonefish but condemned golf as a game for the idle rich. One of his children said that he could never decide whether he owed his allegiance to Greenwich, Connecticut, or

Greenwich Village, New York. A born rebel who loved big words and labels, he was a fine story teller and evening companion at a bonfire with a beer. And our boys loved him dearly.

One of George's idiosyncrasies was his endless passion for building. He came to Barnstable at a time when real estate prices were still within reach of ordinary mortals. As luck would have it he found a sizeable parcel of land close to the shore and bought it at an acceptable price. Then, working with a contractor, he built a house for his family. Time passed and he built a second house shoulder to shoulder with the first. The out building probably came next: it never seemed quite finished. Relentlessly he moved on to a third house which he designed and built in the main by himself. And finally, in a spot with a postcard view looking over tidal marsh to the Harbor and lighthouse, he built his final house where he lived out his days. At some point in this flurry of construction, a grown Warren child announced that his father had an erection complex.

Brook Trout 5 1/2" long carved and painted by George Warren.

But fish were his addiction and passion. Some years before he left us he began making and painting large striped bass. It was a joint project with an old and dear Yale classmate. Then with single-minded, relentless devotion he began carving salmon, trout and bonefish, each painted in spectacular detail, a work product that even Faberge would have been proud to call his own. He turned out dozens of these but commercial success was elusive. However they are and always will be prized possessions of his friends. When the first George Bush was running for President, a reporter contacted Red Dog, Bush's boyhood, school and college friend, and asked for some memories. Red Dog found it excruciatingly hard to say anything that might further a Republican's cause. After Bush was elected, George did send his old friend, now President of the United States, one of his exquisitely carved and painted bonefish and promptly got back an appreciative and charming letter.

Fishing in and just outside the Harbor has been a pleasurable constant for many of us for the last half century. There was a period when we all thought striped bass had joined the passing parade but in recent years there has been a welcome recovery and stripers are back in good quantity. Our oldest son still lives for his trips to sea, now with his brothers and sister and their children. There's nothing like watching a small child trying to land a big fish not knowing which will win. Wading and fishing off the flats in waist deep water is still my favorite. Exciting if you step on a crab and often very productive in front of the Little House with either a spinning or fly rod. Over the years we have turned and painted our own plugs, tied flies and, like most of our contemporaries, we still throw back almost all of the fish we catch. From the log, here are some pertinent entries:

9/16/79 George caught 22 blues yesterday up to 15 pounds each.

8/16/91 Jeb caught a 46 inch bass this morning (before going to work) loose-lining a pogy.

8/30/91 Hundreds of immature laughing gulls trading up and down over the marsh catching some kind of insect. Never seen so many laughing gulls before. Harbor has been full of blue fish marked by diving terns and laughing gulls.

5/22/2000 John Tulp got 35 bass this morning: no keepers.

6/9/02 Fish jumping all around the boat... Grandson Sam had two on.

9/20/03 Bass or blues or both breaking-with gulls and terns enjoying the riches.

6/20/04 Came with Jeb to help watch Brooks and Grace. We went fishing & caught a 41 inch bass. Wow! What a fish. I had lots of fun.

One calm evening Sue and I were sightseeing and casually fishing with light spinning gear. We had caught and returned one small "schooly" and were homeward bound enjoying the evening. On the southwest side of Phillis Island we edged up to a school of pogies riffling the surface of mirror calm water. For amusement I tossed out a small, homemade popping plug knowing that no self respecting pogy would bite it or any other lure. And none did on the first try. Retrieving my second cast, I foul hooked one of the breaking pogies and began reeling it in for unhooking. The quiet and calm were shattered by a great surge and suddenly I was hooked to a sea-monster bass. After a struggle that seemed like half an hour but probably was only 10 minutes we had him by the side of the boat. Gaffless we managed to pull and wash him over the side. For measuring I held him up to my chest and then we set about getting him freed of the treble hooks. He had struck the foul-hooked pogy, now gone, and lodged my wooden plug vertically in his mouth so it was held wide open. Otherwise he would have easily swum off, probably with my plug, line, reel and light rod. We did get him back into the water and he managed to swim off, tired and, hopefully, wiser. By then I was conscious of my own mortality and very concerned about his. We later figured that the long, thin fish measured about 57 inches.

When we could eat the plentiful small bass we caught, fishing was more rewarding and fun. Now we can keep only the bigger "bull" bass, never quite as tasty, and in any case said to be breeding females. If so the conservation rule seems counterproductive. Loose-lining for the big ones or fishing live or cut bait is not as much fun as our old method. At low tide we would wade out a half mile to knee deep water at the edge of the Indian Trail bar and spin or fly fish, often with homemade baits. Caught fish would be threaded on a line tied around the waist, making it possible to fish through the favorable tide without returning to shore. The sensation of having live, swimming fish tied to your waist was unique.

Since fish are tasty and healthful, here is a splendid recipe even if a trip to the market is required for ingredients.

Doris Travers' Fish Chowder (in the oven)

2 lbs. Cod or Haddock fillets.
Put thick pieces in bottom of casserole.
Peel and slice thinly 4 potatoes and lay on fish fillets.
Add celery leaves, bay leaf, 2 1/2 teaspoons salt,
1 1/2 big onions (sliced thinly), 1/2 cup butter cut up
and scattered around, 1/4 teaspoon dill weed or seed,
1/2 teaspoon white pepper, 1/2 cup white wine or vermouth,
2 cups boiling water. Cover casserole and
bake at 355 degrees for one hour. Heat 2 cups light cream
and add and stir with a spatula. Garnish with fresh parsley.

At the Little House we like fillets of freshly-caught blue fish slathered with mayonnaise and cooked on both sides quickly over hot charcoal. Add a crisp white wine, salad and bread and you have a near-perfect meal.

Three foot striped bass by George Warren and John Phinney.

Chapter Twenty Two

DUCK HUNTING

Like the old gray mare, duck hunting "ain't what she used to be". Fewer birds, more restrictions and age all contributed to the gradual decline of the sport as a consuming passion.

But there were several years of ducking in the marsh often on the black banks or islands in front of the Little House. The canoe was put to work again and our big, golden retriever, Buff, was willing company. After the Korean War, contact was renewed with Lee Austin, the retired captain of industry and old family friend. We shot together several times, the two of us, the canoe and big, old Buff. We would paddle out, set our decoys, drag the boat into the longer grass, camouflage it and hide ourselves in the marsh bank. Lee made one unforgettable wing shot followed by a classic leap, splash and retrieve by Buff. While we waited for birds, I heard about Lee's rowing at Princeton, his early bank assignment in Japan, his ride in the late 1920s or early 30s across Russia on the trans-Siberian railroad, his war years and other adventurous times gone by. I found him rare company, one of my deceased father's generation, kind enough to compare my homemade decoys to Elmer Crowell's. Although it didn't mean much to me at the time, Lee with Gordon Marshall owned the Little House but we never shot there or talked about it.

There followed over a period of several years ardent duck shooting along the Harbor shores and in the marshes. One day canoe and I got lost in a sudden fog. It was in December an hour or more before dark when an unexpected and unusual fog set in. My set was on the east end of Little Thatch several hundred yards from the Little House and perhaps a half mile from the Yacht Club where I had embarked. I pulled the decoys and started out in the direction that I thought would bring me home to a drink and supper. I paddled for a long, long time and finally as darkness fell, found myself on the Sandy Neck marsh near Wells Creek on the wrong side of the Harbor. The canoe by that point in its career had become a bit porous so a chance to dump water was welcome. That done, a radio beacon on the mainland side suddenly glimmered in the dark above the fog and I paddled my way home to a bank of car lights and relieved family members.

One cold morning when the temperature was hovering just above zero, I put the canoe in at Scudder Lane and paddled a mile or so out into the marshes to Slough Point. There was lots of ice in and around Spring Creek for fine cover and it was not long before I had my limit. Then down the narrow creek among the floating blocks of ice came a vast raft of sleeping blacks, some seemed close enough to touch and they drifted by while I watched with awe.

Nobody else that I remember used a canoe for shooting: a gunning skiff camouflaged with marsh grass was the usual thing. But many hunters would motor out, hide their boat and snuggle into the marsh bank where the hides were adequate until the tide got too high. Once several of us saw a duck hunter get a deer that had been frightened off Sandy Neck into the marsh.

One day a friend from Rhode Island came and shot from a scull boat, a hunting technique commonly used in Narragansett Bay for blue-bills. His was a recent model in which a single hunter could lie down with his gun next to him and propel the boat by sculling with a single oar through the stern. Rafted ducks are apparently not disturbed by what they must take to be floating debris and my friend spoke about actually bumping into birds in a flock, He did bring back one black that day. Another day he and I used my Boston Whaler to get out to the Little House and the good shooting spots there. It was a fine day with a mild north wind to follow us home at days end when the boat was chock full of decoys and paraphernalia. There being little space elsewhere, my friend lay comfortably across the bow seat of the boat. Somehow when we were probably fifty yards from our home shore we plowed into a wave, the boat filled, the motor died and my friend was out of the boat but hanging on. As he pulled himself back in I stood up and promptly went overboard. Still holding tight to the wheel. I was washed back in with the next wave and we had a cold paddle in and walk along the shore with waders full of ice water. We lost a few decoys but nothing else.

The Harbor has not always been so kind to duck hunters. Taisto Ranta told me about two occurrences when he was the Town's Natural Resources Officer. Both happened in the early

1970s. The first involved three hunters caught on Spring Creek in a flooding tide. One had managed to get to safety on Sandy Neck and he called for help. Taisto was in Cotuit, but picked up his boat and with the help of Eddy Duarte launched it at Navigation Road and got to the hunters. One, the shorter, was standing on a crate to keep from being washed away; the other in water up to his chest was about to lose his footing, and life to boot. Later Taisto retrieved one of their guns, cleaned and oiled it and returned it to the owner but was never thanked. The second involved a man caught in an ice flow east of Scudder Lane. He couldn't talk and ice had formed in his ears. He had to be fought into the boat but eventually lived.

My good friend and contemporary Jerry Cummings was not so fortunate. He was shooting from a gunning skiff over Phillis Island on a clear, bluebird day. Somehow he tipped over, his waders filled and he was lost. Even though it was a mid-day accident and search was commenced immediately by boat and air, it was a year before his body was found deep in the marshes.

Taisto had hunted from the time he was a boy growing up in West Barnstable. But in later life he somehow found himself banding ducks trapped in a small fresh hole off Indian Trail. He said one day as he held one of the birds close to him to apply the band he felt its heart beating and that was when he gave up duck shooting. As I grew older and more conscious of my own mortality, it seemed better to look than shoot. I did shoot a bit with my oldest son around the Little House and there is nothing like seeing the sun rise over a nice set of decoys and watching the morning flights of birds trailing out of the Harbor in skeins miles long. Or watching a wary black scouting you in the fading light of day and then wings set plunging into your decoys. No sport is as thrilling visually.

Flying black duck by Jamie Hand.

Chapter Twenty Three

BIRD NOTES

To keep eyes open and interest at the ready, every house should have a bird list. For bells and whistles, it can be enriched with dates of first sightings and early and late dates when a bird is seen in given years. But apart from being amateur scientists, birds are fun to watch. It's pleasant to greet old friends when they reappear and exciting to discover a new visitor. A list of birds seen in and around the Great Marsh, Sandy Neck and the Harbor by some of the Cape's best contemporary birders will be found at the end of this chapter.

While just plain porch sitting is hard to beat, birds do enliven the scene and add interest. With that in mind and out of a feeling of fellowship, we installed at the marsh's seaward edge a hundred or more yards in front of the Little House a nesting pole for ospreys. This did require calls to the local Conservation Commission because the structure was in a wetland. That approval was forth-coming, subject to Audubon Society consent. There we met some skepticism, but ultimately were given a go-ahead. Shepley's, a local lumber company, donated much of the material.

> 8/11/02 The osprey platform is up. Done in 45 minutes at high tide - loaded our boat with all the lumber pre-cut and organized to erect. Fantastic operation. Here's to many happy osprey families. We had a blast erecting another fine Sandy Neck home.

> 8/13/02 Motored out to check on osprey platform and saw first bird to come in and hover over it. Didn't land but hovered over it twice. Later in our hour stay, the same or another bird paid a visit.

By early October the birds had lined the nest with salt hay and gone south for the season. In March from the mainland we could see the returned ospreys perched on their new nest site. In June when we renewed our visits, there were three vying for the nest site and all seemed shy of our intrusion. That year either no birds fledged or the young fell prey to raccoons or a great horned owl. Courting sleep one night, we heard an owl call in the pines back in the dunes. The next winter was extremely cold and the Harbor filled with great blocks of salt ice which carried away some of the supports for our nest pole. Even though the structure acquired a radical lean, the clump of nesting material stayed and returning ospreys made it their home. One adopted the Little House as its perch and did its sitting on our chimney. Progeny? We think and hope so. There is a pleasant denouement to this chapter of the osprey tale. The next spring before we could act, we discovered that some concerned person during the cold months had straightened the pole and replaced the missing strut: an act of random kindness appreciated by birds and porch sitters alike. We discovered this in early April and there were nesting birds in residence. By the end of May we found two ospreys at the site, sometimes both on the platform and watched one bring a fish to the other. By June a single chick was evident and noisy.

> We have heard that young osprey are inept fishermen.
> 8/23/2005 Yesterday watched young (?) osprey
> catch a fish off Great Thatch & sink into water.
> Once he got it partway out but, fortunately, he finally
> could let go & he and fish each went their own way.

We have heard that once an osprey locks on to a fish it is there to stay. Perhaps, but there must be exceptions or my bird lost its grip. We also think of osprey as fish eaters but once one dropped into a friend's yard with a muskrat for dinner.

In any case ospreys are recommended as a good cure for ennui.

In the fall huge flights of tree swallows congregate on the Neck to fatten up on bayberries and insect protein which they catch coursing over the marsh. We have had flocks appear in early August and found them as late as October but the greatest concentrations are usually in mid September.

> 8/2/81 Tree swallows are everywhere - even flew
> through the porch over our heads this A.M.

138

10/18/02 We have 1000nds of swallows behind
the house on the bayberries - perhaps 10,000.

We have seen the rise in the dune road behind the Little House as evening closed in blanketed with roosting swallows and the next morning found the sand spattered with bayberry pits. Off in the dunes we have watched great billows of birds rise and fall like wind-driven puffs of smoke. Obviously the Neck is a staging area where they prepare for their migration south. One September evening we sailed out for dinner and the night. The next morning dozens of swallows were perched on our boat's peak halyard, the line that runs from the top of the mast to the end of the gaff. When we climbed aboard, we discovered a boat speckled with tiny seeds surrounded by small purple stains. The migrants had filled themselves with tiny wax-covered bayberries, once used to make candles. Birds in these uncountable flocks like minnows in schools can twist and turn in rapid flight and apparently never touch.

While the convening of tree swallows is a natural spectacle well worth seeing, it would be unjust not to pay tribute to their handsome, aerodynamically accomplished cousins, the barn swallows that nest under the Little House. Superlative flyers, they are fast and agile menaces to airborne insects, mixing their quick wing beats with dipsy-doodle turns and swooping glides. Their flying is reminiscent of joyful music played on a lilting pipe: in William Blake's words "songs of happy chear". Setting a barn swallow's flight to music would be a challenging task promising rich rewards.

Migrants and resident birds are road marks on our annual calendar. A January walk can produce unexpected sightings: a living dovekie on the back beach, a short-eared owl in beach grass in the dunes,

...a flicker on porch intent on breaking and
entering. He has left a large bung hole over the door.

Various ruses have been tried to keep flickers from using the Little House as a wedding drum. Time has been our best ally and in recent years the problem has diminished, perhaps with the population of flickers.

Black ducks, countless eiders in great flocks, long-tailed ducks, scoters and Canada geese all winter over in the Harbor as their refuge of choice. Yellow-rumped warblers can be found in pockets of brush in the dunes and brant appear in increasing numbers as the cold months progress. The haunting trumpet of the old squaw on clear, calm winter evenings is one of nature's most evocative sounds. The old squaw has been renamed the long-tailed duck, more descriptive perhaps but less picturesque. Bird nomenclature has become a committee affair to rationalize their names world-wide, an intriguing project not without humor. The suggestion that our robin be renamed the black-headed thrush was apparently voted down, a welcome (and unusual) concession to common sense.

Spring brings migrant shorebirds working their way north from South America to their breeding grounds, often well north of the Arctic Circle. An occasional red knot from Argentina may be seen in passage or a turnstone from Brazil in colorful breeding plumage. The yellowlegs have come and gone by June and have even passed through Churchill in northern Manitoba headed still farther north. Common terns used to arrive to nest just outside the Harbor along with a few roseate terns. That site now is vacant. Simultaneously the migrating bass arrive. The schools of feeding fish break water and drive bait to the surface where terns join the feast. Piping plover and least terns, to whom we owe thanks for limited vehicle use on the back beach, come in March or early April to stake out their nesting territories.

Summer is our time at the Little House to stand watch. Crows that feed in the high marsh are lively, intelligent and welcome vis-itors. One summer in North Harwich I bought a young crow fresh out of the nest but close to fledging. After a week or so on a dog food diet he learned to fly and became a daily source of amusement. When I rode my bike down to the culvert pool he would follow me flying from telephone pole to telephone pole cawing, wildly pleased with his worldly travels. Every boy should have a pet crow and we have had several. One was almost scalped by wild crows that seemed to consider the domesticated bird either a territorial invader or outright traitor. Crow pets today are probably illegal.

Willets, large handsome shorebirds which breed locally, appear to be thriving. We see them regularly beginning early with continued sightings throughout the summer.

*5/13/99 We watched a willet this morning on
a neighboring dune, king of the mountain.*

*7/26/02 The willets treat us as interlopers. I
find them good company . . .
Willet beside himself: sits on top of roof or in
the marsh in one place scolding constantly.*

That year a crotchety willet with a raucous voice spent the summer scolding us whenever we dared trespass near what he considered his Little House. Possessive watch-birds like this we take to be breeding residents and they are gone from the dunes and roof top by early August. We find flocks of a dozen or so usual in September on the east end of Great Thatch.

*7/28/91 We saw a huge flight of willets - 75 to a 100 over
Green Point - a first for us along with the summering eider.*

The dramatic pattern of the willet's flashing black and white wings and their piercing cries make them stand outs and sassy favorites.

Some eider, mostly immature, do stay through the summer. Perhaps these are non-breeders or, in the case of mature birds, cripples. One year some were found dead on the beaches, possible victims of the "red tide" ingested from their mussel diet.

Less popular are the mobs of cormorants that collect near the aquaculture grants. One can speculate whether the grants are the real draw; but in the 1940s there were virtually none to be seen in or outside of the Harbor even in the fish weirs. Cormorants in the last half century have become common in Barnstable like other thriving newcomers including cardinals, mocking birds, titmice, snowy and great egrets and, most recently, oyster catchers and red-bellied woodpeckers.

Late one August we had two northern harriers: one was a male, perhaps young because he never seemed as sleekly silver and black as the mature adult; the other perhaps a juvenile female. It was delightful watching the long-winged birds chase and apparently play with one another sliding low over the marsh then gracefully tilting and floating sharply upward. Growing up we called these birds marsh hawks. The name change is perhaps justifiable internationally to avoid confusion with other raptors, but it is a mouth full to apply to our old friends on Sandy Neck who for years have shared with us their airborne rapture. It is always a thrill to watch the larger and more common brown and cinnamon female soaring low over the dunes and marsh. We have often wondered why these birds course and hunt the high marsh so close to the water's edge where no mouse (at least not one with a tide chart) would dare go. Recently a woman told a group of birders that she watched a marsh hawk take a yellowlegs, a good sized shorebird. Other noisy yellow-legs took up the chase and eventually the caught bird broke loose. Marsh hawks are ground nesters and must be vulnerable to the raccoons, coyotes and foxes that inhabit the Neck.

With August comes the bloom of the new bait-fish crop and a feeding bonanza for birds and fish alike. Many entries in the log refer to the feeding terns funneling over bait driven to the surface by bass and blues. Laughing gulls, grown-ups and young, join in to participate in the feast.

September brings Indian-summer, clear blue skies scoured by the north wind and whimbrels, sometimes single birds, once a flock of a dozen or so in the long grass by Bridge Creek deep in the Great Marsh. These are our curlews, big birds that winging by with their long down-curved bills look like refugees from an oriental painting.

In recent years we have had many great and snowy egrets from late August into October. In the 70s and 80s snowies seemed more common but recently great egrets have become more prevalent. Both are striking members of the heron family that show brilliant white as they float on wide wings over the still-green marsh. One day in 2005 as we cruised along the black banks up Harbor we counted over 35 in pods here and there. Numbers of great blue herons also populate the marsh in September and October. They are big and angular, their lumbering flight and hoarse croaks suggesting some

Great blue heron by Jane Layton.

prehistoric creature. Closing my eyes, I can see their broad, black-tipped wings rowing through the air low over the marsh.

10/3/02 *Migrating blue herons throughout*
the marsh. One just cranked a greeting.

October brings the blacks, the skunk-heads (eider to most), the geese, coot (known in the books as scoters) and our other winter residents.

11/3/01 *There's a great flock of black ducks between Phillis*
and the Yacht Club must be a thousand plus or minus.
We flushed them from the corner east of the house.
Also some buffle-head, eider and a pintail foursome.

The days shorten, the marsh turns gold and we humans migrate to our fireplaces.

Every year produces unusual sightings. In January of 1973 Peter Auger in the course of his 40 days on Sandy Neck had the thrill of spotting and watching a sand hill crane. He wrote in his contemporary thesis:

"I spotted the bird as I was working my way towards the point of the Neck…I recognized it as being the slow, graceful beat of an unusually large bird. In fact, as it neared, I couldn't believe the size of the magnificent creature…I guessed its wingspan to be over five feet.

Landing about two hundred yards from my vantage point, the tall grey bird lifted its head, extending a long, slender neck….I watched as the bird took numerous short hauls over a period of about a half hour….During these runs, the intense flapping needed to get the bird's huge body airborne immediately petered out into a slow, sweeping glide back to earth… [a] beautiful example of avian aerodynamics…"

Only once going to the Little House have we happened upon

7/29/02 *…six or eight storm petrels on the way out.*
"mother carey's chickens" dancing on the water.
Fabulous. A large pod of whales beached in Dennis
today – Jeb called and hoped we'd help!

Not trained, we let Jeb down that day. Whether the petrels in the Harbor bore any relation to the whales beached in Dennis we'll never know.

One fall after a long storm red-necked phalaropes appeared on Cape beaches and we, without glasses, saw a phalarope swimming in circles in one of the flooded areas in the dunes. The red-necked phalaropes, pelagic birds that live their lives mostly at sea, had come from off the African coast and were blown far off course on their way to their Arctic breeding grounds.

Often in the fall gannets come into the Harbor. They too are pelagic birds that can convert salt water to fresh and come ashore primarily to breed. Long-winged gliders they spot their prey from high in the air and plummet straight down with locked wings and shock-resistant heads throwing up tall plumes of spray. High drama watching gannets fish. But October of 1991 brought Hurricane Bob and days of driving winds from the northeast. Afterwards a half dozen were found on the back beach, victims of the high winds or their own inability to get airborne again. Unusual sightings, such as the peregrine sitting on the back beach at the Point or the black terns we see each fall migrating south from Canada, do add spice to our lives.

Why birds? That is a common and fair question usually posed by a skeptic. Three reasons come to mind. Birds are fascinating, beautiful and rewarding.

People have been intrigued by bird migration since the beginning of recorded history. It is well-known now that swallows don't bury themselves in the mud to winter over. But how do migrating knots find their way from the high Arctic to Argentina? With many species, the adult birds fly first, leaving the young to fend for themselves. Instinct must play a role. Another piece of the puzzle is needed to explain how homing pigeons taken 1000 miles away in a box find and return to their roosts. Or how terns taken hundreds of miles in dark confinement when released find their way back to their nest sites. And how do migrants know when to fly and in what direction and why do they bother? Fascinating, and the more we know about the life histories of given species, the better we can identify and admire the real world travelers like the Arctic tern. Its round trip flight is some 25,000 miles each year from the high Arctic to the Antarctic via Africa and, sometimes, Sandy Neck.

Bird flight is another subject of long-time interest and study. Poor Icarus before his final swim learned that wings of wax had serious shortcomings. Until the Wright brothers, there were probably many other futile attempts to imitate bird flight. Watch a barn swallow or chimney swift and try to imagine how man could possibly duplicate their everyday flying. In *Log Book for Grace*, Robert Cushman Murphy wrote "I now belong to a higher cult of mortals, for I have seen the albatross!... even more majestic, more supreme in its element than my imagination had pictured...as it turned and turned, now flashing the bright underside, now showing the...upper surface of the wings, the narrow planes seemed to be neither beating nor scarcely quivering. Lying on the invisible currents of the breeze, the bird appeared merely to follow its pinkish bill at random." An albatross was recently seen off Sandy Neck by an equally excited observer. Another incredible flying machine is the ruby-throated hummingbird that doubles its full weight to 1/4 of an ounce in preparation for its long flight across the Gulf of Mexico. Its total migration route from South America may extend north some 3500 miles. Over the years, many have found bird flight a tonic for the soul worthy of wonder and contemplation.

That birds are beautiful is self-evident. Gould, Lear (who wrote about the owl and the pussy cat), Wilson, Audubon and many other artists have devoted much of their lives to capturing on paper the brilliant colors, elegant shapes and infinite variety of birds. Sit on our porch and watch the swallows and, no matter how blasé you are, see if you don't recapture some of the wonder of childhood. We all know that the beauty of bird song is one of life's unique joys. Shelley wrote about his skylark "Hail to thee, blithe spirit". There are no skylarks on Sandy Neck, but there are mockingbirds which sing with unequalled exuberance and variety. What a delight it would be to be able to identify all of our local songsters by their voices alone. One expert, now deceased, is said to have mastered and retained 4000 bird songs.

But how are birds rewarding? Our reactions are the rewards and nothing more is required than interest and looking: no looking or interest, no rewards. But once you have identified a bird you have made a friend and meeting friends always gives pleasure. When you are in Africa and see a barn swallow you can smile to yourself and say "I know that bird". Old familiars are old friends and new birds are new friends, the more the merrier.

Birds add a dimension to travel. Wherever you travel you will find old and new friends and looking for them is a nice way to spend a free moment. Listing what you've seen should not be the sole object but it tends to stimulate interest. A house list like ours for the Little House keeps one looking for new finds; and records of past sightings with dates can provide interesting comparisons. But there is more to the enjoyment of birding than keeping lists. We humans like company, common interests and doing things together. When you and several others go exploring to find birds and suddenly someone makes a good spot, all of you will feel a wave of shared pleasure and that shared enthusiasm is the reward that makes birding such a popular outdoor sport. Good birders help others see and identify and both the helping and being helped involve rewarding human interactions.

So the real question is "Why not birds?" They are beautiful, interesting, challenging to find and identify, good adjuncts to travel, pleasant to share with friends and they have the miracles of color, song and flight: in short they are good companions for day-to-day living. Anyone who is indifferent to these cohabitants of our planet doesn't know what he (or she) is missing and is the poorer for it.

One fact is certain: they have added untold pleasure to our moments at the Little House.

Following this you will find two lists. The first is from our log, a one day illustrated list done by an appreciative visitor. The second is a compilation of sightings by Greg Hirth, Stauffer Miller, Blair Nikula, Robert Pease, Jeremiah and Peter Trimble, and Mark Tuttle, all recognized to be among the best of contemporary Cape birders. For more details including dates and nesting data, the reader should refer to *The Birds of Sandwich & Barnstable on Cape Cod Bay* by Robert Pease published in 1985 by The Wayside Studio.

A Day's Birds (from the Log)

15 Aug. 2002

1. Semi-palmated plover
2. " sandpiper
3. Sanderling
4. ruddy turnstone
5. black bellied plover
6. willet
7. least tern
8. Common tern
9. laughing gull
10. herring gull
11. ring-billed gull
12. black backed gull
13. great blue heron
14. tree swallow
15. barn swallow
16. piping plover
17. great yellowlegs
18. lesser yellowlegs
19. Am. goldfinch
20. Snowy Egret

BARNSTABLE BIRDS OF HARBOR AND NECK

Note: This list includes sightings made by of a number of people over a long period of time. The areas covered are the Great Marshes, Sandy Neck, Barnstable Harbor and contiguous land, flats and water.

Red Throated Loon
Common Loon
Horned Grebe
Red-necked Grebe
Northern Fulmar
Greater Shearwater
Sooty Shearwater
Manx Shearwater
Wilson's Storm Petrel
Leach's Storm Petrel
Northern Gannet
Great Cormorant
Double-crested Cormorant
American Bittern
Great Blue Heron
Great Egret
Snowy Egret
Green-backed Heron
Black-crowned Night Heron
Yellow-crowned Night Heron
Mute Swan
Brant
American Black Duck
Canada Goose
Mallard
Northern Pintail
Greater Scaup
Common Eider
Harlequin Duck
Long-tailed Duck
Black Scoter
Surf Scoter
White-winged Scoter
Common Goldeneye
Barrow's Goldeneye
Bufflehead
Hooded Merganser

Common Merganser
Red-breasted Merganser
Turkey Vulture
Osprey
Northern Harrier
Sharp-shinned Hawk
Cooper's Hawk
Red-tailed Hawk
Rough-legged Hawk
American Kestrel
Merlin
Peregrin Falcon
Ring-necked Pheasant
Northern Bobwhite
Clapper Rail
Virginia Rail
Black-bellied Plover
Lesser Golden Plover
Semipalmated Plover
Piping Plover
American Oystercatcher
Greater Yellowlegs
Lesser Yellowlegs
Willet
Whimbrel
Hudsonian Godwit
Marbled Godwit
Ruddy Turnstone
Red Knot
Sanderling
Semipalmated Sandpiper
Least Sandpiper
Dunlin
Short-billed Dowitcher
Common Snipe
Wilson's Phalarope
Red-necked Phalarope

Red Phalarope
Pomerine Jaeger
Parasitic Jaeger
Laughing Gull
Bonapart's Gull
Ring-billed Gull
Herring Gull
Glaucous Gull
Great Black-backed Gull
Black-legged Kittiwake
Royal Tern
Roseate Tern
Common Tern
Arctic Tern
Forster's Tern
Least Tern
Black Tern
Black Skimmer
Dovekie
Thick-billed Murre
Razorbill
Black Guillemot
Rock Dove
Mourning Dove
Great Horned Owl
Snowy Owl
Short-eared Owl
Belted Kingfisher
Downy Woodpecker
Northern Flicker
Willow Flycatcher
Carolina Wren
Marsh Wren
Sedge Wren
American Robin
Gray Catbird
Northern Mockingbird
Brown Thrasher
Cedar Waxwing
Northern Shrike
European Starling
White-eyed Vireo
Yellow Warbler

Yellow-rumped Warbler
Pine Warbler
Prarie Warbler
Common Yellowthroat
Northern Cardinal
American Tree Sparrow
Chipping Sparrow
Field Sparrow
Savannah Sparrow
Grasshopper Sparrow
Salt-marsh Sharp-tailed Sparrow
Seaside Sparrow
Song Sparrow
Swamp Sparrow
White-throated Sparrow
White-crowned Sparrow
Dark-eyed Junco
Snow Bunting
Red-winged Blackbird
Eastern Meadowlark
Common Grackle
Brown-headed Cowbird
Orchard Oriole
Northern Oriole
House Finch
Common Redpoll
American Goldfinch
House Sparrow
Great Crested Flycatcher
Eastern Kingbird
Horned Lark
Tree Swallow
Bank Swallow
Barn Swallow
American Crow
Black-capped Chickadee
Tufted Titmouse
Blue Jay

Rare Sightings
Yellow-nosed Albatross
Pacific Loon
Sand Hill Crane

Chapter Twenty Four

DUNE BEASTIES

White-footed wood mice are cute little devils and regular squatter tenants of the Little House. One day early in our tenure we paid the house a visit. When we opened the storm door, there between it and the inner door was a lovely, soft-lined nest filled with squirming baby white-footed wood mice. That day we closed the door and came back to the mainland. Who could disturb such a peaceful domestic world of what Robert Burns called "wee, sleekit, cowerin, tim'rous beasties". Sensible creatures like wood mice cherish unoccupied houses when brisk weather comes.

Like any shred of wilderness left in our densely populated world, Sandy Neck has its good share of animals, great and small. One night, before the house was elevated, several of us sat eating when a red fox trotted across the porch. We asked him in, but he declined. Perhaps he was the same fox we found asleep on one of our long walks in the middle of the Neck where people seldom tread. He or another often left us messages on the porch. In earlier days my Grandfather hunted fox on horseback on the Neck. A group of riders would start at the Sandwich end and drive the foxes toward Beach Point and the lighthouse.

In the evening we have found skunks scuttling along the wrack looking for tasty treats served up by the last high tide. Skunks are common on the Neck and on the Cape. Our North Harwich house had a lighthouse cellar with a small window at ground level for light, an eight or ten step ladder down from the living room, and it was empty, most of the time. It was called a lighthouse cellar because it was round, about ten feet in diameter, and had brick walls. A skunk must have found the window open and been curious. In any case, there he was in the morning on the basement's dirt floor pacing round in circles against the cellar wall. We called a neighbor who knew about things like skunks in lighthouse cellars and he came to the rescue. He lowered himself slowly down the ladder, stepped to the wall's edge and waited for the skunk to continue its methodical rounds. When the skunk walked between his legs, he lifted it by the tail, climbed the ladder and once outdoors dropped the critter into a burlap bag. Both departed leaving the house, scentless and brimmed up with a respectful, admiring audience. Skunks we were told can't produce without their feet on the ground. If the same rule applied to legislators, we might live in a better world.

There are many deer on the Neck but they are largely nocturnal skulkers, not often seen. Several years ago one of the Rangers told me there were about twenty resident deer, all does, and that the bucks came only when the does were in rut. One winter day when we walked the several miles home from the Little House we were followed by a pair of deer. They stayed just over the dune line that paralleled our path and watched us with only their heads bobbing up from time to time. We could almost overhear them sagely agreeing that the devil you know is better than one you don't know.

Another time in the early evening we were putting around in our small boat when something unusual by a marsh creek, just out from the woods and dunes, caught our attention. We approached slowly and as quietly as we could by outboard, and when we were ten or fifteen feet away up came the long ears of a little spotted fawn, left there apparently for safekeeping. After it lowered its long ears we saw it no more despite its proximity. Our dog, Braley, then a floppy, Yellow Lab puppy, caught our excitement and with nothing much in mind (a not unusual state) jumped ship and was so unsettled by his first swim that it took all we had to pull him back aboard. By the time he had been retrieved and finished shaking and dousing us, the little fawn had disappeared.

A further word about Braley who now manipulates us with consummate skill and no sympathy. Mostly he likes to eat and knows that we hold keys to the larder. He sports a typical juvenile's sense of mischief, greeting us always with something in his mouth, generally an attention catcher he knows he shouldn't have. But it was through Braley that we did have a memorable meeting with a family of Sandy Neck neighbors. He was probably a high-spirited yearling at the time. We had walked over to the big cranberry bog behind the Little House and part way out to the back beach. It was a glorious day, bright sun but pleasantly cool. We were high on a dune ridge watching Braley below us entering bushes at a bog's edge. Sue was the first to spot the line of five coyote pups exiting from the same bushes about 50 yards to Braley's right. Then several hundred yards across the bog emerged first one then another adult coyote. Both stopped and watched us from afar. We called Braley who came back having registered no interest or excitement and together we started the trek back to the Little House. Normally Braley can sniff and spot a potential canine playmate miles in the distance: but this time there was no interest. After we had come down from the dune ridge and walked several hundred yards we heard barks and howls. Looking back there was one of the adult coyotes exactly where we had been, open and silhouetted against the sky, wolf-like and awe inspiring in this remote place. Braley, who does like dogs for company, never looked back. He must have understood clearly that this particular neighbor did not appreciate his presence. The coyote population is a somewhat recent phenomena. In spite of hunting they do survive and help control the Neck's mouse, rabbit and deer population.

Everyone with a remote gunning camp, like the Little House, needs an advanced degree in raccoon-proofing. Raccoons are intelligent and when winter comes prefer a snug, unoccupied cabin with comfortable mattresses to a wet hole in a windy tree. And they are accomplished at breaking and entering down chimneys or through freshly chewed holes. A friend, clever and inventive with patents on beer openers and things like that, was plagued by a mob of local bad-boy raccoons. With some respect he told me once that he could never invent a latch for his garbage can that the raccoons couldn't open but his garbage man could. Sensitive to political correctness, he made it clear this applied only to his garbage man, not to garbage men in general.

I have known many raccoons both as pets and as pests. In the early 1940s comic books had back pages with enticing advertisements for secret rings, turtles, chameleons and other things that appealed to children. One advertiser was a fur farm in Lacrosse, Wisconsin. Thinking that an otter might be a good bedfellow, I sent for the list of available animal children. It came offering a great variety but no otters. A bear cub for $35 seemed a bit expensive and my limited reading about bears suggested that age might make them unruly. So I settled on a $6 raccoon. Along he came on the 4th of July, 1941. He was in a rectangular five gallon tin can with a hole in its topside covered by a jury-rigged wire door. Mother and I could hear him moving around in his tin house, possibly upset after his long trip to Cape Cod from Wisconsin. With courage that now seems admirable, we finally managed to release the gate and eventually a bright-eyed, masked face popped up to survey his new world. In no time he was scrambling around the room inspecting every crack and corner and winning our hearts with his plaintive chittering. Ultimately he climbed all over us and decided we were acceptable parents, under the circumstances. We named him Chichi, short for *Otshi Tshornye*, dark eyes in Russian from the folk song of the same name. In a different world, every child should have a pet raccoon, but they do bring heartbreak. Chichi quickly became housebroken and never failed to amuse all with his antics. He walked with us, swam with us and followed his curiosity into every corner of our world. Although he had had a rabies shot, sickness came at some point in the summer and impaired his ability to use one of his hind legs. We learned that it was rickets and a pediatrician friend prescribed vitamin D which he had daily from that time on. He continued to be the family favorite until late in 1941 when he got into ant poison and could not be saved. Chichi and his successors added a priceless dimension to growing up.

A number of pet raccoons followed, some much more successful than others. A kit bonds to human foster parents immediately and parades along in their footsteps wherever the footsteps lead. One who had never seen the ocean followed me in one morning for a swim, with no hesitation whatsoever. They swim well and naturally. We did see one trapped by an incoming tide on Great Thatch Island out in front of the Little House. He probably swam the necessary several hundred yards to safety on the Neck. Years ago we could get a permit to keep a raccoon pet but probably for the best that has now changed. When raccoons reach maturity they become testy and unmanageable and therefore troublesome pets. An adult "domesticated" raccoon that wanders into a neighbor's house can become frightened and dangerous. One other fact about these engaging animals, at least in an enclosed area, they get along well and like to play with dogs. On the other hand there is no love lost between raccoons and cats which immediately jump ship if a raccoon enters the room.

So much for the pet side. We learned about the pest dimension at the Little House. We always know raccoons are nearby because of the calling cards they leave on the porch and the plank bridge used to cross our mosquito ditch. And over the years our dogs have squared off at night with raccoons exploring the salt hay wrack at the high tide mark.

Chamois faced up to a big raccoon at the marsh edge in the middle of the night. Lots of barking and a willing retreat when called.

Thatch has just cut a raccoon off from the woods & driven him into a ditch where he decided barking was the safest offense. What a happy [and smart] dog.

With dogs, too, discretion is the better part of valor.

But our Sandy Neck neighbor raccoons have gotten much more close and personal than that. Over the years we have provided rent-free, comfortable winter accommodations for a number of raccoons, usually discovered on our first spring visit. They have come down the chimney when the damper was not closed or closed tight. While easy to house break as pets, our uninvited guests have tended to think a winter trip outdoors unnecessary. In May of 1994 we found a mother and three babies who left and stayed out after we closed and weighted the damper. In early June of 2002 we evicted a mother and baby from the attic. A second baby was left behind dead in a smelly house.

If you are thinking about your own remote getaway, you should know, and perhaps you do, that raccoons can be very frightening. When surprised and cornered they let out a banshee scream and bluff a charge. If this is unexpected you may be surprised, not only about the raccoon, but also about how far you can jump.

In the course of one first visit of the season, I had fumbled around in the house for some time and raccoons were far from my mind.

Deciding to take the mattress cover from the top bunk bed in for a washing, I lifted the mattress and there under the bed spring a couple of feet from my nose were a sleeping mother and three bright-eyed cub raccoons. Mom had apparently had a hard night on the town.

154

Thank goodness! I had no appetite for facing off at eye level with a cornered mother raccoon and her threatened triplets. The mattress was dropped back into place posthaste. Our eviction technique is to install a boom box with the volume turned high and leave it over night

Enough to keep man and beast at bay.

And always it has worked. This particular raccoon had chewed her way in through the roof so maintenance was required to slam the door in her face. Usually the problems are more serious and extensive.

Never mind what wild raccoons think when the weather gets cold, they are not welcome guests at the Little House!

Raccoon by J. J. Audubon.

Chapter Twenty Five

SANDY NECK HOMESTEADS

The Latin term "sui generis" means one of a kind or unique and it fits perfectly most of the Sandy Neck dwellings. In the cottage colony at the Point there are 33 structures with beds: on the marsh trail which runs along the south of the Neck to the blacktop road there are 24 more, for a total of 57 in the 6.2 mile stretch. And they come in assorted sizes and shapes much as they were originally built with whatever was available, without "improvements" and the guidance of today's building codes. And they are passionately cherished by their owners. Four of the houses on the marsh trail are more than a hundred years old and shed some light on the use of Sandy Neck over the last century.

Closest to the access point at the west end of the Neck is the "Marsh House" built around 1896 by (or for) Frederick Lowell and his friends Lyman Dyer and Joseph Sargent. Mentioned above in Chapter Nine, it is a compact, one-room gunning camp well and solidly designed and built with a porch. Mr. Lowell's brother, who also used the camp, was Guy Lowell, the architect who designed the Boston Museum of Fine Arts, the Unitarian Church in Barnstable, the New York County Court House and many other public and private buildings. Perhaps the Marsh House was one of his early works. Another user was Edward S. Holmes director of Boston's Museum of Fine Arts. The men were said to have loved their shack more than their wives. Over time the owners acquired some 20 acres of marsh in and around Marsh Camp which the Town in 1962 took by eminent domain awarding $2190 for the land only, so the building now stands on Town land and is leased to its present occupants. This land and most of the west end of Sandy Neck was originally owned by the Bodfish and Blossom families, both early Barnstable residents. John Bodfish was the Lowell predecessor in title and his is a story that deserves further study. He went blind in his early 20s after serving as principal of the Osterville Grammar School. Subsequently he entered and graduated from Boston University School of Law, became the Barnstable

Town attorney and was known for his speaking ability, his writing and poetry. He recognized the recreational possibilities of the Neck and in 1920 deeded two acres of beach to the Town "to see that all had public access to Sandy Neck and Cape Cod Bay." It was this first step that encouraged the Town to acquire in various takings substantially all of the remaining Sandy Neck land.

The "John B. Rogers Cottage" is a mile or so further east along the marsh trail. It was originally built prior to 1892 as a cranberry storage house and living quarters for cranberry workers. In recent times it has been substantially changed. One of the additions was constructed using rough three inch square lumber washed up on and salvaged from the back beach. The lumber was transported to the house by a Model A Ford with sand tires originally used by the Coast Guard. Town records indicate the lot on which the building stands was originally described as a "12 load piece at Dimmock's Cove" which meant the lot yielded 12 wagon loads of salt hay. John Rogers along with Braley Jenkins, Francis Gorham and Charles Bassett were the major early cranberry growers on the Neck. The remains of the bogs and dikes along the south of the Neck can still be found, but difficult access and storm driven salt water made them unproductive and impractical and they were ultimately abandoned.

The "Halfway House" built before 1872 is situated farther east about halfway out the Neck. It too was built as a cranberry house for storage and living. The original one room building has been extended by wings to the east and west. Owned since shortly after the Civil War by the Stevens family, the structure was given to the Town by Clarence and Olga Stevens with the understanding that it would be used "...for conservation purposes and to further educate children through exposure to the multiple resources on Sandy Neck. Through their generosity students and scientists are using this cottage as a base camp while doing field research and observation to learn more about the wildlife that inhabits Sandy Neck and The Great Marshes."

The "Bishop/Fogarty House", located across the Cove from the Cottage Colony at the Point, was built around 1875, was often remodeled and has now been replaced by a modern two story summer house, probably the most recent construction on the Neck. That it was permitted came as a surprise to many. The original house was an outstanding example of whimsical design done free of restrictive rules by an inventive fire chief from Onset named Clayton Bishop. Mrs. Fogarty, the remarkable woman who spent 50 years on Sandy Neck, lived out her late summers alone in the original, remote structure.

The Cottage Colony, anchored by the lighthouse at its east end, progresses westerly with its 33 dwellings mostly shoulder to shoulder along the beach to the slightly removed Barnacle at its west end. With the exception of an occasional off-season visit, the houses are used primarily for vacationing in the warmer months. Once the lighthouse was erected and the keeper's house built, the colony grew in fits and starts until development was halted by lack of land and restrictive building policies.

The land at the Point, known as the "60th Lott", was allotted in 1715 by the Proprietors to Joseph Lothrop and Ebenezer Lewis and by 1829 was in the possession of Ebenezer Bacon. He sold two parcels, one in 1829 known as the Provincetown lot, and then he or his successors granted small parcels for cottages. Many titles on Sandy Neck are difficult to show conclusively because some deeds were not recorded, some claims are based on possession and many of the original stakes, trees and markers have been washed away or moved. Like the bound that ended at the stake in the ice, the stake in the sand was not much better.

In 1826 the Town deeded the lighthouse property to the Federal government. While that deed survived the 1827 fire, title records do not show how the Town acquired its ownership. The present lighthouse replaced an earlier light on a tower atop the dwelling of the first keepers. The present brick tower was built in 1857 45 feet above the ground and 33 feet above mean high water, close at the time, according to my Grandfather, to the end of Sandy Neck. As accretion extended the Neck toward Dennis, in 1931 the lighthouse was replaced by a steel tower some 200 feet closer to the end of the Point. In the early 1930s the brick lighthouse was decommissioned and sold with the keeper's house to private owners. In 2007 the bonnet was replaced and its flasher added so the old and well-known landmark now looks much the same as it did when constructed in 1857.

The first keeper's house was replaced by the existing Victorian structure in 1880. It is solidly built for winter living complete with gingerbread and Palladian windows. Its design echoes that of other similar facilities built for lighthouse keepers along the east coast. During World War II the house was turned over by its private owners to the Coast Guard to use as headquarters for men training on the Neck. At one point there were as many as 16 occupants. During this period the first (and for years the only) phone on Sandy Neck was installed in the keeper's house.

Sandy Neck Light circa 1900. Salt print courtesy of Sturgis Library.

Lighthouse as it appeared 1934 to 2007.

Sandy Neck Light after 2007 restoration.

The Cottage Colony did grow steadily in spurts. Structures have been torn down with new ones built from the leavings of the old. Outbuildings have been converted to dwellings. The difficulties of obtaining and moving materials have encouraged economic and functional design. One boyhood friend described the colony as Cape Cod's only rural slum but he was wide of the mark. Like another New Englander, the residents are delighted to simplify, to live life deliberately, to hold change at bay and to know that they have tasted life to the bone. Of the existing dwellings other than the keeper's house, five were built before 1900, five from 1900 through 1910, four from 1911 through 1919, fourteen from 1920 through 1939 and only four from 1941 to date. The most recent new construction was in 1971 and it replaced another cottage that had fallen into serious disrepair. In 2007 a shack was moved to the Colony from its original westerly location on the Neck.

Four of the surviving buildings built before 1900 shed light on Cottage Colony development. Starting at the west end the cottage one in from the Barnacle known as "the Sunset" was originally the kitchen ell of the Barnstable Harbor House restaurant located at the other end of the colony. On privately owned land, it was probably moved by the Lovells to its present location around 1910. "Hurricane" is located about in the middle of the beach front houses and was built in 1898 as a gunning camp. Story has it that construction was in process at the time of the Portland Storm hence the name "Hurricane". The gale, high tides and massive waves took out many trees, stakes and markers confounding many Sandy Neck real estate titles for all times. The addition to the west began life as a hen house. The cottage called "Comfort" is located behind the beach front houses and is thought to be the oldest on the Neck at least in part. During the Portland storm the occupants of Comfort were taken from a second story window and rowed to the lighthouse on higher ground. The kitchen portion of Comfort is believed to have been the office for the four whaling try-yards reserved by the Proprietors in 1715. Whether the kitchen portion was built on this site or moved is not known. In the early 1900s Comfort was used as a gunning camp. The "Barnstable Harbor House", located next on the beach to the keeper's house at the east end of the colony, was built prior to 1888. It was here that Benjamin Lovell and his son, Herbert, ran the restaurant described in an 1888 newspaper article "Near the lighthouse Mr. Benjamin Lovell of Yarmouth has a cozy restaurant near the beach, which is a favorite with all summer sojourners as well as the people of Yarmouth and Barnstable. Associated with him is his son Herbert. They also carry on quite a fishing business in the vicinity principally with nets. Some twenty-five can be seated at the table in a dining room that is always cool, and served with a chowder, baked clams and a seaside dinner that cannot be surpassed. Mr. Lovell is adept in the art and was a pioneer in putting in cans the well-known Lovell's Clam Chowder. Guests from the Nobscussett House and many other points visit Mr. Lovell's Barnstable Harbor House in yachts and a light wharf for their convenient landing has been constructed. Over the restaurant are two comfortable sleeping rooms for the regular occupants or accommodation of sportsmen but no pretense is made to 'keep a hotel'." Close your eyes and think about being sailed out to the Point on a hot summer day in one of the great catboats for a fine clam and lobster dinner accompanied by stories of hunting, fishing and days at sea told with relish by an old salt. The Harbor House restaurant closed its doors around 1900 and the building was sold by the Lovells in 1936.

In 1915 Shirley Lovell married an English registered nurse named Constance Prowse and he and Davis Holmes, a Barnstable housewright, built for winter living the "Big House" on land leased from the Bacons. It had plastered walls, a fireplace in the living room, a wood and coal stove and many of the comforts of contemporary homes on the mainland. In 1920 Shirley's brother, Leston Lovell, with Davis Holmes, built the "H. Leston Lovell House" also winterized. Both of these Lovell houses were on the beach at the west end of the clustered houses. Shirley and Leston and the light keeper and family were the only winter residents of the Cottage Colony. They mended nets, repaired lobster pots, built houses, laid in provisions, guided and set out duck hunters on the Neck and in the Great Marshes and, probably, shot a bit themselves. There is a colorful description of coot shooting with Shirley and a stay on Sandy Neck in *A Book on Duck Shooting* by Van Campen Heilner. Constance was a fine cook according to Mr. Heilner. In the summer months the two brothers with their fishing boats kept the cottagers in food, drink, ice and supplies.

In the late 1920s Constance started the Sandy Neck Camp initially so a few city children could enjoy nature at first hand. Like many worthy enterprises it grew and grew and grew accounting for five of the 14 houses built from 1920 through 1939. This was the boom period for construction in the colony. At its peak, the camp had 155 children, 25 counselors and various helpers and 12 of the colony's 33 dwellings played a major role in camp life with the Big House being the hub. Quoting the 1929 prospectus for the camp: "Sandy Neck is a beautiful clean sandy stretch of land, dotted with sand dunes, low grasses and patches of pine woods, away from the dangers that lurk on the mainland, where automobile traffic is a constant menace to life and limb." The camp continued to afford pleasure to children until 1957. The next year the Lovells converted the camp buildings to summer rentals except one which floated across to the mainland in a heavy 1958 storm.

The Lovells and Davis Holmes working together or separately built seven of the colony dwellings and probably worked on many more.

After negotiations broke down, the Town in February of 1975 condemned the Bacon land at Sandy Neck comprised according to the Order of Taking of approximately 144 acres. The offered award was $230,000. Litigation ensued and was finally settled in 1981 for over $1,000,000 which included interest and payment for additional acreage which had accreted since the surveyed plan referred to in the Order of Taking. The taking applied to land only, so occupants of the buildings on the former Bacon property have since leased their sites from the Town.

Of the cottages in the colony, each has its story to tell. The most recent, the Annex, replaced a run down structure built by Francis Manning Hinckley who in his day was master of *Arabia, Ocean Queen, Winged Hunter, Star of Peace* and *Leading Wind*, all ships in the far eastern trade. Mathias Hinckley, who raced the *Mail* against Yarmouth's *Commodore Hull*, was Francis M. Hinckley's father. Three cottages in the colony, one a home-made house trailer, were built elsewhere and hauled in by Jeep or other vehicle. Several were moved back from the beach to allow for construction of a bigger house (the Pratt House, for example, with its two floors and four bedrooms). Another was floated on two dories around the Point from the back beach with never a broken dish despite a five-week delay in transit while Davis Holmes' injured hand repaired. Many were built as gunning camps. One floated over to the mainland in a storm and seems never to have come home. On the other hand one was floated over to the Neck from the Common Fields in Barnstable. Some were built on site with lumber brought over by the Lovells. The cottages came or grew in various ways in all sizes and configurations.

The colony is anchored on its west end by the "Barnacle" built by Davis Holmes and his sons in 1936 for Richard Cobb and his wife. Mr. Cobb was headmaster of Milton Academy in the early 1900s. Town records quote these two entries from Mrs. Cobb's log.

"Sept. 21, 1938 - A dry southeaster in spite of which Betty Davis and I brave wind and sea and with six baskets etc. and 50 lbs. of ice. Arrive at the little house wet and happy with only the loss of my old brown hat. All snug and tight within but a sandstorm outside. Unpack lunch make beds sweep and settle ourselves comfortably. Bless Herbert for lugging us over and rescuing Betty from a tight squeeze wedged firmly with feet in air and helpless between cabin and rail".

"Thursday Sept. 22, 1938 - The little house whining and shaking a night of hurricane, but staunch and snug a beautiful morning after the storm. Fresh southwest wind and cloudless sky. A rough swim but warm air. Went to Mrs. Lovell's for dinner and were greeted by tales of disaster and destruction which she had heard over the radio. Tidal wave at Onset House washed into the canal at Bourne. Electric service disconnected. Railroad bridge gone at Buzzards Bay, no train service and the Cape cut off from the rest of the world."

The 1938 hurricane has seldom been described so casually.

Henry and Patsy Kittredge bought from the Cobbs in 1945 and Henry's sister, Dora, named the cottage the "Barnacle", a perfect name that has stuck down the years. Henry was headmaster of St. Paul's School in Concord, New Hampshire and was one of Cape Cod's best known historians. He loved the Barnacle and used it from time to time for duck shooting. Somewhere I once saw a photograph of Henry, Alfred Redfield and, perhaps Marcus Howes, all in gunning gear sitting on the porch of the Barnacle.

For six generations, the Lovells have lived at Sandy Neck and shared their lives there with many other people. We all owe them a debt of gratitude for helping to make it and keep it as is.

Duck hunters on Sandy Neck and, perhaps, an early look at cottage colony.

Chapter Twenty Six

MEMORABLE MOMENTS

Sedentary creatures now and then need a bit of adventure. Climbing Everest (cost $60,000 or more), racing around the Horn or just sailing around the world in one's own boat, all are beyond the reach of most of us. But those of us tied to desks or fettered by commitments crave change and excitement.

Whenever we drop the mooring line to our sailboat, even for a short sail to the Little House, the unpredictable possibilities for minor trouble hover over us like evil spirits. The nice, fresh breeze can poop out, a Grandchild can remember something long forgotten at home but now critically necessary, the dog can go overboard, a hat can blow off and be elusive to fetch or a cold squall can make the short trip wet and less than wholly pleasant. Then when we arrive the process of anchoring the boat so it won't be high and dry at departure takes thought, imagination, skill and (even) luck. Judging from the log, a recurring problem seems to be making the anchor line fast.

> But, despite warnings, Bear throws anchor before attaching rope to boat, so both anchor and line go under with boat adrift. Oops!! Bear makes a quick dive and recovers. So much for valet service. (Steve Nill).

Little adventures, yes, but often sufficient. For night arrivals the yawning potholes add excitement.

> Very entertaining upon arrival when Matt fell into a pot hole while carrying 2 sleeping bags and a pillow. The gear stayed dry. Good save!

Mind you these happenings while exhilarating are not life threatening and we consider that a plus. Not being too good at our primal activities adds a touch of zest and helps avoid lives of quiet desperation. The little challenges that interrupt well-laid plans, sudden unanticipated changes of circumstance, a contrary mother nature can all be aggravating, exciting and refreshingly different from daily routine.

Lovely night under the moon. No boat in the morning.
Walked home. Found boat next to Town beach.
Ho hum.

Sitting here on marsh, after countless games of Uno,
contemplating the Whaler which will be sitting on the
marsh for another 12 hours at least. Tied up to stake
overnight with a very short line & plenty of water. This
morning went to move the boat out deeper ... and found
ourselves beached. High tide was at least 1 1/2 feet
lower than last night. Now it's pouring. (Steve Nill).

My chair collapsed last night. Must have been
something I ate.

Fine dinnerware left on table (two forks and a spoon)
were hand-hewn from driftwood upon our recalling
that all flatware went south for cleaning. Oops.

Adventures or misadventures, who cares. These tests of resilience are one of the charms of a visit to the Little House.

When you clamber out of the arm chair and turn off the television, or leave the lawn mower or golf clubs and head out in your boat to Sandy Neck, you are going to a different world. You step out into primordial ooze that squeezes between your toes, scramble up a slippery bank of marsh peat and walk to the house along a muddy path with soft spots and prickly marsh grass to accelerate progress. Once, just when we got close to the house at the edge of the marsh, a small snake slithered into the windrow of salt hay along the high tide line, only once in our almost 30 years. So one comes to a different world with different concerns and rhythms.

We had a great walk in the dunes & watched
the first stars come out, then returned to the
cabin...It was quite windy, so I worried a little
about rattling noises and things blowing, before
settling myself into the sleeping rhythms of the cabin.

The vistas are of big sky, water, grassy islands, acres of marsh, green brush against white sand dunes and the solitary, weathered Little House boarded up against raccoons and other uninvited guests. For maximum enjoyment it is desirable and necessary to give yourself to and become a part of this different world, to be absorbed by it. And over the years we and our guests have learned different ways to do this.

> Early in the morning we lay on the big dune behind the house and listened. We heard mocking bird, song sparrow, airplane, gentle surf and Sue slapping gnats.

Years ago when the flood tide was at rest, I swam the mile or so directly across the Harbor from the Yacht Club with an 18 or 19 year old girl friend of one of the boys. She could move and stopped half way on Phillis Island to hustle me along. Her encouragement failed and she did the final stretch in cold water in jig time leaving me far behind. That was a more difficult swim than the several miles out to the Point with the tide when it flows fastest. Someone once told me the tide accelerates and ebbs on a flow rate scale of 1-3-5-5-3-1 but here there are complications due to the sand bars and shape of the Harbor. Somehow a long swim and perhaps even a short one off the marsh helps to draw one into the different worlds of Barnstable Harbor and Sandy Neck.

> Came over about five in a strong west wind arriving at high tide. Swam around the estate beginning at the west pool (where the water was warm and delicious) and worked our way from there into the big water (delicious and cold). Attacked by three quahogs, two of which we ate in self defense, with drink. The third repented and was put back.

And so does a long walk following the road along the marsh and then crossing the Neck in the pine woods to the back beach, then backtracking along it and finally crossing the dunes to the Little House.

> Molly [the dog] and I walked across to back Beach while Janet stayed and read her book. We decided to walk back via the woods where we came upon an observation hut...Proceeding down into thick brush we scared up a large doe which then hoofed its way out of our sight. By and by we came upon another hut only to discover

that it was the one we had seen. Unknowingly we had made one large, complete circle. We collected our bearings and headed off again. In the next 30 minutes we stumbled upon a red fox, what must have been an enormous owl, several cranberry bogs and finally the back beach. We'd done it again! This time we walked down the beach until I knew we had a clear shot across the dunes to the cabin, where we found Janet peacefully reading her book...(John Lay)

Janet added

I didn't even know they'd left!

One evening son Seth took a two hour walk around the point.

Mom told me to start on the back beach because otherwise it's hard to know where to cut across - good motherly advice that I followed. There were quite a few campers on the back beach, which surprised me. But a good distance around the Point was roped off to campers and horses. As I walked I saw folks either leaving or nestling in for cocktails. It would be a great night for a bonfire over there. After resting a bit on the Point - and taking a few swigs from my water bottle I headed to the houses and the road running along the Harbor side. That was clearly the highlight. Beautiful meanderings around the inside of the big, green salt marsh at Mussel Point that were glistening in a spectacular light. The road turns through the forest - a magical stretch where I saw a deer and hoped for a coyote...When I came out of the forest to the marsh there was a deer standing out in the middle of it. I watched it apparently feeding for a while . . .When I came back out to the marsh the deer was running across it and leapt into the forest.

And another time son Ned reported

We walked through the western woods & saw a field mouse (or maybe it was a small coyote).

Once we too came upon a fox sleeping on a bed of pine needles under one of the old stunted pitch pines, very peaceful. We left him asleep. Another time we jumped a great horned owl that glided along in front of us from tree to tree until he tired of our company. The woods have a magic, elfin quality with wind-cropped trees and ground cover of pine needles, hudsonia and lichens reminiscent of high elevations in the White Mountains or arctic tundra. The woods can be maze-like.

> Lyn and I got disoriented in scrub pine, sweated profusely, found agua - lolled in green water. Whole experience primitive and therapeutic - great contrast from urban southern California.

Although there may be a rare walker or jogger, still these long walks can be and usually are experienced alone or with friends, providing opportunities to be absorbed into this special world. One man we met was running around the whole Neck, more than a dozen miles, training to run up Mt. Washington.

Once I walked alone several miles from the Point down the middle of the Neck, skirting cranberry bogs, catbrier and patches of bayberry, blueberries and heavy brush. The sand was hot as it is at midday and I remember a brown thrasher teed-up and singing and a single cedar waxwing with the yellow tip of its tail showing bright in the sunlight. Brown thrashers, once common, today are not. Sometimes when one walks and lives this way the mundane world dissolves and the dunes, the grumbling surf and the wind whispering in the pines take over: a rare and profound experience when this happens.

One afternoon we sat at a dune top at the level of the pine canopy which we could just about touch admiring the sand that fell at its steep angle of repose to the tree's base. We watched a little warbler, olive-backed and yellow-bosomed, that hopped restlessly through the pine boughs at eye level only feet away. Real novices in those days we were delighted to get back to our field guide and discover we had been watching an aptly-named pine warbler plying its trade. Time out to watch is good medicine.

Fishing is another way to shuffle off the burrs of daily living; best when you slip out of the boat with a fly rod and wade on sand waist deep in the shallows. The inlet in front of the Little

House is a natural bait bowl and in the fall can erupt with small blues and stripers. At mid-tide the water is only two or three feet deep and with light wind it can be a fly fisherman's paradise.

And there's always the primal pleasure of treading up quahogs.

Another way to attain the nirvana that Sandy Neck can be is to sit on the porch and watch the clouds drift by and the tide slowly flooding or withdrawing from the marsh in front of the house. Sometimes it comes right up and licks at the steps but not rambunctiously enough to damage the steps, or one's trance.

No jeweler could ever have found a better setting. Under all that sky are the vistas of marsh fading off in the distance in the west; the ever-changing Harbor to the south; to the east more marsh, a glimpse of pine woods and miles away the toy lighthouse at the Point; and the backdrop of pristine dunes. Looking east and west from the porch, the sunrises and sunsets are outstanding. At night, away from lights of the mainland, the stars shine with an almost forgotten splendor. Late one summer across the marsh and water we watched Orion rise in the east, long before we could see it from our house on shore. When we sleep on the porch we often roll over in the dark and look across the still Harbor to red-lighted radio towers and a few twinkling lights reflected in the mirror-calm, ink-black high tide. There are many tributes in the log to the light and colors

> dramatic dark clouds and spot lights of sun on the dunes. ...I can hear a train back in the real world, otherwise all is crickets and wind.
>
> In the morning the sun shown through clouds and dark shadows raced across the green-gold marsh. The colors everywhere are subtle and spectacular - patches of golden rod at the marsh edge, brilliant red patches of salt wort in the marsh, clouds of small purple asters fading to white, the poison ivy - mahogany red - and the glorious white sand crested with tasseled plumes of dune grass.
>
> Tide's beginning to slip away in a gentle drizzle - all gray and coppery with the marsh burnt gold & the water silver to leaden.

170

Blues and purples and pinks...the most spectacular lighting of the season

Gorgeous clouds & colors on the dunes - a superb treat for the eyes and spirit.

I woke early to the sounds of chirping and the pink and golden light of the rising sun. The water shimmered and glowed, glimpsed just beyond the vast green of the marsh. A magical hour.

The blues and the greens and the sun and the breeze - pure bliss.

It is a beautiful, perfect late summer evening. The sun is slowly sinking down...the marsh is green as only it can be, and the sky is blue, fading to its deeper blue high above where a half moon floats. The Harbor reflects that blue, blue sky.

First visitors feel the magic . . .

Providence and Washington seem a long ways away.

This place is really another country. This morning. so quiet, just crickets and frogs chirping, gulls calling...

...a real paradise and a view to treasure forever.

A painter's paradise - every view a picture waiting to be painted.

What a beautiful, calming place!

It's a gorgeous day with a very light wind and we have all we can see to ourselves, except for the toy sailboats way over the Harbor.

In short, the Little House is in a world of timeless, breath-taking beauty: a calm refuge from life's turbulence.

One windy night I

Came back alone by canoe at low tide, my first solo. But I wasn't really alone. There was a moth and a big harvest moon that came up like a bubble out of the dunes. And there was a bone rattling west wind.

171

Most of us are not entirely alone very often in our daily lives especially in a remote marsh location where the nearest trace of civilization is a mile or more away. The shutters banged in the wind, the house squeaked and made its own music, and it took no imagination to hear the patter of little feet above my head. And who or what might be walking the sandy trail right behind the house? The truth is that solitude ratchets up one's sensibilities. And solitude we have to spare, alone or with one's lover or wife (hopefully the same) or select friends. Of course, solitude means different things to different people. This log entry memorializes someone's visit on August 27, 1978:

> Swimming all the time. The only piece of dry clothing was my bathing suit.

Being isolated from life's usual interruptions magnifies each moment and impresses them indelibly in memories and hearts. Sounds, like the breaking waves on the back beach, the horned owl's "ho-hoo-hoo", the plaintive voice of the black-bellied plover, or in the fall the silence-splitting quacking of a black duck, or the cricket's chirp, all become part of a natural symphony never to be completely out of mind. And the same is true of human voices, if there isn't too much tinkling of ice or clattering of silverware.

> As I sit here at the table in the dark, there is only one sound, the wind... It's the next morning and I am here all alone: time to myself. Still I hear big winds. Air New England commuter to Boston just flew over - it's 7:25. And now sun peeps through grey clouds. The birds see the sun and start to sing and fly. A swallow on the chimney sings a song -- a beautiful one. And now I hear a Bob White just to the west. (June Warren).

> Am I at the little house on the prairie or something? This makes lonliness seem nice. (L. Cummings).

> Another glorious night of marital solitude. ...A meal, a walk. A visit from a friendly skunk. Awake to see the moon blush and set. Back to sleep. A much needed dose of togetherness.

172

Its solitude is part of the magic of the Little House. It's all so simple, the porch and the tiny frame structure. Described by a friend

Mountainous sea sand
Bold ship of weathered shingles
Swimming on the wind

Walking down the sand road at night and catching a flicker of light from the window reminds one of how important and precious to we humans shelter is. It is almost beyond belief that a pair of squatters lived in the house throughout one or more winters. But a roof over one's head and female company tend to make the world a tolerable place. Once we found this note scribbled in barely legible pencil on the porch.

7/13/91
Hi! Thanks for the use of your lovely porch during
a rain storm. We love your house. A clam digger

Any port in a storm? They had found a special one!

Being at the antique structure begets curiosity. A Grandchild will appear with a small bit of whale bone or, perhaps, a flake of quartz or a possible arrowhead. Out in the marsh are stubs of weathered pilings and several are still to be seen near where we anchor in a small canal-like opening that reaches closer to the dunes. In the house itself we have found an old wooden case, empty, marked on the end in concentric circles "Booth & Co. London Finland Superior Gin old Tom" and on the sides "Gold Medals Calcutta 1885 New Orleans 1884-1885", a hand made yoke for a man to carry pails of water, an old metal wheelbarrow, odd bits of wrought iron, some crude decoy bodies with separate and equally crude heads, a set of metal shore bird decoys neatly nested together and an empty smoke bomb used for target practice during World War II. There is much here to be seen to tickle the imagination and fuel inquiring minds.

He who sits and overlooks the marsh is privileged to a preview of dog heaven. Over the years several Labs have shared our moments on the Neck. When we go to the Little House we take the dog, space and company permitting.

First came Chamois, a big dog devoted to the pursuit of birds and butterflies, he loved the fresh water bogs found in low places in the dunes.

173

Last night he chased a swallow across miles
of green velvet. The swallow thought it was
fine fun & so did we.

Chamois - A water dog - loves to retrieve:
1) swimmers; 2) boats; 3) paddles. Last night
we sailed & eventually came to shore. Good south
west breeze. Sue threw the anchor, including the line,
and we drifted gently to the opposite side of our creek
that runs to the dunes. Chamois harassed the entire
operation. I threw a paddle to Sue which didn't get there.
He retrieved it & then swam in circles trying to decide
which of us to favor. Finally he chose Sue & was
rewarded with a "Good dog!", a historic first.
   A bird dog - chasing has now progressed to shore
birds. He runs for miles never pausing when he plows
into a ditch or sinks into shoulder deep mud.
   He does grace our scene.

   Chamois, as usual was a damn nuisance but had a
lovely time.

Next came Thatch. He too endlessly enthusiastic loved chasing
birds across the meadows but was a bit high strung and finally
suffered a sad, accidental death.

Thatch lives every minute as if there were a squirrel in it.

Here in a major gale - just as we got in the cabin
the rain started. It hasn't let up but for a few moments
since - and the wind is fantastic... We made grilled
salmon in the fireplace and drank some champagne
while Thatcher shivered in fear of the lightning &
thunder. One burst of lightning seemed right over
our heads.

Two later entries

For Thatcher this brings back puppy hood... Despite
back legs that don't work, his nose still does & only
he knows what the winds bring standing here looking
at the sunset.

Poor Thatch is in dog heaven - we hope and pray.

The author and Thatch in living-dog heaven.

Then came Braley, named after Braley Jenkins, the early cranberry tycoon who claimed ownership of most of Sandy Neck. Braley first came to the Neck as a puppy and everything there was and still is an adventure including wallowing in the muddy ditches, digging in the sand, falling overboard and bringing us the remains of long-dead critters. Still a juvenile delinquent, when he gets to the Neck he sometimes prances rapturously in circles. He swims: all Labs, designed for swimming, have webbed feet. Best of all, he likes to eat and sniffing the high-tide hay line is his preferred pastime looking for old, delectable, often very ripe, morsels to roll on, chew or share with us. As one visitor observed

> Braley, the dog, constant menace to the food.
> Much character. Very imaginative beast.

The story of young Braley's meeting with the coyotes is told elsewhere.

It is exhilarating to see a house-bound dog free to run, sniff, swim and explore at its pleasure. A treat to watch them chase low-coursing swallows across the salt meadows, crashing into the mosquito ditches, sending up great geysers of spray and finally returning, all tail wags and filled with pride about the bird almost caught. Before our ownership of the Little House came Buff, a leonine Golden Retriever who took to retrieving ducks like a professionally trained wonder dog. We spent many a cold morning in the canoe together and he would eloquently register disgust when I missed a shot, as I often did.

We cherish the notion that the boundless joy of our dogs at being free in this wild and wonderful place is contagious, and for those of us who are dedicated members of the dog-lovers fraternity, in fact it is.

In the family, the Little House has become the place to celebrate special occasions, anniversaries, birthdays, bachelor dinners and for our married offspring getting away, with or without children. Now that we have more than 50 behind us, the anniversaries spent at Sandy Neck stand out, often because of ineptitude and moments of high comedy. But always the cooking worked out and all that followed was memorable. Our children have honored the precedent and made the Little House a kind of one-night-stand specializing in anniversaries that often seem to occur on dates bearing no relation to wedding dates.

> May 12th. Came with canoe, champagne and porter house to celebrate 28th. Strong SE wind made paddle over stimulating. About 10-20 seals watched our passage by Great Thatch with good-humored interest. Last week the grass was dead and colorless: this week the grass has tinged the marsh with green....Starlings in chimney provided odd musical accompaniment to a delightful morning with grapes, bacon, eggs & a touch of bubbly champagne.
> It's a nice world.

Birthdays provide another reason for private and special celebrations for young and old, and there seem to be lots of both. The little ones love to take their friends to the dunes and introduce them to their own special and private world and we can tolerate being alone and celebrating in our own way. This is the reaction of a young visitor from Germany:

> We have celebrated my thirteenth birthday...on Sandy Neck. I can say with full truth that it is the most delightful party of my life.

The house has survived several bachelor dinners. The aborted pig roast has perhaps been covered elsewhere unless good taste or sense prevailed. But there was one misty morning after one of these long evenings when we decided to go out and view the chaos. Out of the fog emerged a boat draped with corpses heading back to the mainland and aspirin. Then the rain closed in coming at us across the water and only later did we learn that all survived as did the Little House, perhaps even more of a miracle. Our troops are older now and this animal-house nonsense should be spared us all, at least until the next generation.

Worthy of note is the single honeymoon spent one June at the Little House:

> It was wonderful out here as always. We had two days of rest after a spectacular wedding. After some mix-up with the sailboat, we left the Yacht Club at about midnight in a dark-of-the-moon high tide & with just enough light to see the outline of the house from about 75 feet off the marsh. Once we arrived we lit a fire & settled down to champagne and a great night's sleep.

So here's to the Little House which, standing alone, has helped many pursue happiness and realize the joy of life.

Photo courtesy of Michael Segar.

177

Chapter Twenty Seven

A LOST ART?

The last chapter overlooked comfortable contemplation, a source of pleasure and inactivity favored particularly by elders. In these days of fast food, hip hop and sound bites, relaxed sitting is on the endangered list. In the interest of recreational rest, here is one man's recipe for a good sit. These are the essential ingredients and at the Little House they abound: quiet except for the voices of nature; an inviting chair; unscheduled time; rare to infrequent interruptions; a handsome and changing prospect; a cordial climate; a book to read or pretend to read; sustenance; and good company or none. More details are set forth in the following paragraphs.

Start with a comfortable chair. We have a couple of outdoor, rugged rockers and several canvas director's chairs that we move to the porch on arrival. It's nice to have variety in case some irritant, like restlessness or a wife for example, provokes a change.

Peace prevails at the Little House and lazy leisure thrives on peace. While total silence generally contributes, the sounds of crickets, distant waves on the back beach, shore-bird calls and whispering wind provide a lulling backdrop of natural music.

Interruptions should not be tolerated. Time cannot be your master if the sit is to be of highest quality. Sometimes wives, children or dogs think that the here and now is the only time to accomplish some trivial thing. They should be trained to recognize and accept the likelihood of other and better times.

A pleasing prospect is another key ingredient, and the porch of the Little House affords that to a rare degree. To the right is the vast salt meadow, of varied textures and greens in the summer and rich golds in the fall, laced in all seasons with changing threads of silver water as the tide ebbs and flows. To the south and directly in front are some of the "haying fields" and almost a mile of Harbor interrupted by Great Thatch and Phillis Islands. To the left our boat bobs at anchor. In the distant south the hazy skyline is Cape Cod's backbone of glacial moraine. Then at the far left we have still more marsh, dunes and the open water that floods in and out around Green Point.

One defense against unwanted intrusions is a book in one's lap for quick reference if pressures to move threaten to become irresistible. If guilt beats an incessant drum on the sitter's conscience, as a final resort he or, to be politically correct, she, can turn to list making. Writing down things that need to be done seems to have a soothing effect on restless observers. The few projects we have at the Little House once listed tend to drift by or be tabled for further consideration.

When we sit there are many gentle and restful things to captivate our eyes, ears and minds. Watching the tide creep to the flood and then gradually recede over the marsh is a satisfying natural rhythm useful for setting one's inner clock. Sometimes with highest tides the water comes under the house so one seems to live in a floating world. This was not such a pleasing prospect to the two girls on their independent project when they first discovered themselves surrounded by water. Little did they know then about the extent of Barnstable's tides. Perhaps they imagined that they might drift away like Noah with no one in their ark but themselves, a baby raccoon and the resident wood mice.

Our tides are worth watching! On the south shore of the Cape the rise and fall averages around three feet. In the Harbor mean tides are almost ten feet. We have been told that tides operate in great saucer-like basins and that ours are in the Maine tidal basin which effects northern Massachusetts, the Maine coast and even the Bay of Fundy. At low tide we cannot get to or from the Little House by boat. There we live by a tide clock which provides generous time for sitting and waiting.

179

One evening when the tide was running particularly high, we sat having our day's-end drink and spotted an empty skiff, cross-harbor and adrift. For sitters it provided a changing source of eye-catching interest. The wind was from the southwest, steady but not offensive. First we watched the runaway hang up on the grass tips of Little Thatch Island perhaps a half mile to our southwest. Then the incoming tide flooded the grass and the skiff was adrift again. At this point we probably refreshed our drinks and sat again to watch the unfolding drama. Soon our feature performer fetched up on the high marsh three or four hundred yards to our front. And the tide continued to rise. To the best of memory darkness fell, we had supper and soon we too drifted, in our case off to sleep. In the morning we found the lost skiff quietly resting at the foot of our steps. No one ever claimed it and it was given to a neighbor, a fruit of the rolling sea. This recollection is recited to show that prolonged observation can produce surprises and be quietly productive, wives' notions to the contrary notwithstanding. Of course not everyone can have as a sitting aid a runaway skiff with a come-hither instinct. Something that catches and holds one's interest makes sitting seem more worthwhile: a rewarding illusion. In any case that was a perfect instance of a high-class and rewarding sit.

The spectacle of flying birds captures attention and offers rich possibilities for productive thought. The buoyant flight of swallows, their ability to fly wing tip to wing tip in changing clouds never touching, coursing harriers floating down-like over the marsh, the black and white flicker of a willet's wing, the croaks of great blue herons and their ponderous, prehistoric flight, the brilliant white of the egrets, the honking of migrating geese in the fall and the honking of mating pairs in the spring, all enliven the moment and transmute it to a treasure well-worth hoarding and cherishing. Where have these wild creatures come from? How do they find their destination? The things we can see and the things we don't understand all deserve recognition and contemplation, and both are aided by sitting.

A big sky with a few fleecy white clouds sliding by is balm for the restless soul. Sometimes cloud shadows race over the water or across stretches of marsh. Or highlights flicker across the dunes or the distant mainland. Racing sailboats across the Harbor flying colorful spinnakers are diverting splashes of color. And of course when you're just sitting on a porch, there's no need to clamber to the other side of the boat or dry off the salt spray. High level activity has its place, but from the sitter's viewpoint meditation tops participation.

As we sit we can look across the Harbor and almost hear the busy hum of men. Most of the far shore is now developed although several extensive tracts have been given to conservation groups for preservation. Today's phenomena are the mega-houses constructed on postage-stamp sites often to replace the more-fitting, modest originals. These immodest starter castles, that result perhaps from tax laws or serve as balm to owners' egos, are the products of newcomers who do add to the tax base and, in the long run, may bring substantial change to more than the face of Barnstable. Sitting on our porch we can see development happening; we can question the roles of zoning and historic zoning; and, perhaps for the better, we cannot see the future. The Little House, almost 100 years old, will continue to provide a place for sitting and contemplating as long as God wills.

Full and comfortable chairs engender quiet talk and new opportunities to be cordial and strengthen friendships. Sometimes there's the rare passerby to share a word with or to speculate about. Occasionally we are blessed with a story teller. George Lyman Kittredge, Harvard's great Shakespeare scholar, lived in Barnstable and his grandchildren are wonderful raconteurs. Whether we first heard this tale sitting on our porch at the Little House or elsewhere makes little difference: it is the kind of anecdote that spices life. Way back when Professor Kittredge was teaching, Harvard had a policy that if five (perhaps it was seven, but that's incidental) students wanted a course Harvard would provide it. The requisite number asked for a course in comparative religion and President Lowell tapped Professor Kittredge for the job. Story has it that the good professor studied for the summer, gave the course and never went to church again. Story tellers that can shed light on human nature or the world around us are warmly prized on our porch.

And finally as day ends one can watch the sun gradually sink below the horizon marking the end of another peaceful day at

Sandy Neck. Sitting has these several virtues: the chairs get dusted off; drinks and meals taste better; relaxation gently settles in; and the magic carpet of sleep comes quickly and helps bring sweet dreams.

Sitters viewing the Harbor circa 1895: a once and always pleasure.

PART SIX

Afterthoughts

"Over incresaingly large areas of the United States, spring now comes unheralded by the return of birds, and the early mornings are strangely silent where once they were filled with the beauty of bird song."

Rachel Carson *Silent Spring* (1962)

Try Yard Meadow and the Little House.

Chapter Twenty Eight

PRESERVATION

One day in the 1960s a well-informed neighbor told me that various people in the Town were considering the possibility of a black-top road running the length of Sandy Neck. Thankfully, that has not happened yet.

We owe the pristine quality of the Neck today to diamondback terrapins, piping plover, least terns and a number of dedicated individuals concerned with the future.

Barnstable and Wellfleet Harbors constitute the extreme northern range of the diamondback terrapin. In the late 1800s and first decades of the 1900s terrapin soup, said to have been a tasty delight, was treasured by gourmets. One can picture large-bellied men with big mustaches and diamond stick pins slurping turtle soup laced with sherry. During the turtle soup heyday, many barrels of terrapins were shipped from Barnstable to New York, Baltimore, Philadelphia and other urban markets. Mrs. Lincoln in *The Boston Cook Book* (1894) writes about terrapin. "This expensive member of the turtle family is highly prized in Baltimore and Philadelphia, but seldom used in New England. Terrapin may be kept alive through the winter by putting them in a barrel, where they will not freeze, and feeding them occasionally with vegetable parings." Her recipe calls for sherry. *The Cookbook of "Oscar" of the Waldorf* written in 1896 includes a recipe for terrapin soup. On the other hand none is found in my 1997 edition of *The Joy Of Cooking*. Styles and tastes do change. Turtles were increasingly scarce and that essential ingredient, sherry, was a victim of prohibition so turtle soup tended to drop out of style allowing the few survivors to live on in Barnstable.

Diamondback terrapin are an endangered species under Massachusetts law. The discovery of nesting terrapin in the dunes coincided with a practice that more and more people recognized as dangerous and abusive to Sandy Neck's fragile ecosystem. Driving all terrain vehicles in the sand had become a cult sport and rolling over on steep dunes was considered the be-all (if not the end-all) by some. While considerable political heat and controversy was generated, in due time regulations were crafted that sharply limited vehicle traffic and, incidentally, afforded protection to breeding terrapins. The current several thousand, while less than the Harbor population that preexisted turtle soup, is still a credit to enlightened laws and regulations and to the individuals who fought for their survival.

How effective have the protective actions been? In the early 1970s the terrapin population was around 1,000. By the 1990s the count had increased to 2,500. The current population is projected to be 3,000 to 4,000 but an updated count is needed. The Marsh Trail has been reopened and increased aquaculture has resulted in more boat traffic, both potential causes of increased turtle mortality.

Piping plover and least tern, both beach nesters, were blue-listed from 1972 until 1985 when the U.S. Fish and Wildlife Service listed the plover as "Threatened" in New England and the tern as "Endangered". The "blue list", prepared and updated by National Audubon Society since 1971, provides early warning of bird species with diminishing populations and ranges. The back-up data for blue-listing is a resource used by U.S. Fish and Wildlife Service which is responsible for determining "endangered" and "threatened" species under the 1973 Endangered Species Act. Both categories are entitled to protection under Federal law. The population of piping plover in the Atlantic Coast Region had dwindled in 1986 to less than 550 pairs and least terns were almost completely eradicated by plume hunters. Beach traffic and use was one cause of the decline, loss of habitat another. Both species nest on Sandy Neck and today nest with a good rate of success because of traffic and use restrictions carefully imposed and well monitored by Town rangers and Audubon Society volunteers. The restrictions enforced during the breeding and fledging seasons have curtailed beach buggy use and vehicle access to the cottage colony at the Point with the incidental effect of preserving to some extent even in heavy tourist months the wild and open character of Sandy Neck's back beach. Because terns are colony nesters that nest in groups, they are easier to protect than piping plover that pair off and nest separately all along the beach. Controls have not been readily accepted. Bumper stickers proclaim that piping plover taste good and cottage users have threatened litigation to prevent any impairment to their access to the Point. At least for the time being a balance has been struck relying on alternate routes and a requirement that passage through the nesting areas be guided. Young plover are precocious but they, like terrapin, can get caught in deep tire tracks and run over. Considerable efforts are being made for plover to avoid this too common fate.

So restrictive laws and regulations have helped to save both least terns and piping plover on Sandy Neck. Since 1973 breeding pairs of least terns there have increased from a low of 15 to a high of 399 in 2007, with variations from year to year but the trend is clearly upward. The results for plover are the same with the low number of breeding pairs three in 1988 and the high of 33 pairs in 1992, again with variation from year to year and a clear upward trend. There are now about 550 breeding pairs of piping plover in Massachusetts, about the same number as there were in 1986 throughout the entire Atlantic Coast Region.

Turtles, plover and terns alone could never have stopped the abuses and over uses of Sandy Neck: it took brave, concerned and dedicated people. Not all the benefactors are known to the author, but here are a few who deserve praise and thanks.

Taisto Ranta, the long-time Sandy Neck ranger, should be singled out. Over the years he did apprehend abusers but much more important in many instances he helped and encouraged people to understand and appreciate the Neck's special qualities.

Rob Gatewood, Administrator of the Barnstable Conservation Commission, has monitored projects and shaped policies and regulations that have helped to strike a balance between appropriate use and preservation of an area of spectacular beauty not so different today than it was five hundred years ago when it was occupied only by native Americans.

Donald Griffin (1915-2004), a nephew of Alfred Redfield, grew up in Barnstable and cherished it throughout his long and productive life. Listed in *Who's Who in America* as a zoology educator, he graduated from Harvard in 1938, earned his MA and PhD there and by 1953 had become a Harvard professor. Subsequently he became a professor at both Cornell and Rockefeller Universities. A world leading expert on bats, he and another scientist first discovered that bats used echolocation. In his later years he became concerned with the question of whether animals could think and plan. During his last years he worked closely with a group of teachers and college students on Sandy Neck participating in various projects and experiments. Whenever he had a question, he would start by saying "Well you probably know a lot more about this than I do..." Of particular interest was a study house for bees seasonally located for several years in the middle of the Great Marsh. He told the author about one experiment that intrigued and amused us both. Bees do have many fascinating and unique attributes. It had been said (using my own numbers) that if a food source was put 50 feet away from the hive, and then after its discovery moved another 50 feet in the same line, and then to 150 feet in the same line, bees would be waiting for the next move at the 200 foot mark. I have picked arbitrary distances and intervals. In any case the notion was tested and Professor Griffin seemed satisfied that the last food source was discovered not by extrapolation but by efficient explorer bees whose job it was and for centuries has been to find new food sources. In any case this brilliant and modest man worked with local students and teachers encouraging and nourishing the hunger to learn in many. In the course of his Sandy Neck work, he became a mentor for Peter Auger.

Peter Auger graduated from Barnstable High School and in 1973 from Amherst College intending to become a doctor. His college honors thesis, *Sandy Neck Journal*, tells of the 40 days he spent in a gunning camp on Sandy Neck from late December of 1972 through January of 1973. He opens his journal with these words: "Ever since I have known it, I have been enthralled by Sandy Neck. Located on the northern side of Cape Cod, the Neck is a vast, beautiful area largely untouched by man and his society." And these words are from his postscript: "Having been exposed to Nature in this stark, intimate fashion, I have been able to discover and experience feelings that I hadn't the faintest idea existed within me. The most important experience of my life..." The seeds for a life-long commitment to the Neck had been planted.

Instead of going to medical school, he was persuaded by the principal of Barnstable High to teach biology for a year and help coach baseball and football. Remembering his college thesis, he was intrigued with the idea of using the Neck as his classroom. Taisto Ranta told him about an old abandoned cranberry house owned by the Town that might be fitting and available. All the required arrangements were made and for almost 35 years Peter has used the building for field biology courses for high school and college students. In 2005 over 200 students participated. And what have they learned? The terrapin story is told above. Peter and his students played a key role in effecting the protections. Over the last 25 years they have put collars with radio transmitters on 20 to 25 deer and seen the population grow from one or two deer in 1980 to the present level of around 40. The herd does require management but over-hunting threatened its viability. The resident deer are primarily does; bucks go ashore for richer food sources and return during rut. The first coyotes were trapped and collared in 1995. They have four to five puppies and a very extensive range that stretches far beyond Sandy Neck. Six years before coyotes were trapped and collared, foxes were. When the coyotes came, foxes disappeared but now they have returned. And the students have constructed a significant data base for diamondback terrapin, piping plover, least tern, raccoon, skunk and the other resident plants and animals of the Neck. Somewhere along the road, Peter got his PhD and 12 or more of his students have done the same. Eric Strauss was one who signed on as a Sandy Neck ranger and later did his dissertation on piping plover bringing to bear his extensive field experience. He is now a biology professor at Boston College.

But perhaps the most important result of these years of dedicated service is the growing constituency of individuals who have experienced Sandy Neck and shared its wonders. These are the people who down the years are best suited for and will help to preserve and perpetuate its natural sanctity and beauty.

So the turtles have won the race for Sandy Neck, with the help of a couple of small birds, the Federal and State governments and some brave soldiers to espouse their cause. At least for the time being they have won: but the pressures can only increase and, if we are not careful, we human rabbits may still end up with the prize and put a black-top road down the middle of the dunes and through the pristine, quiet pine forests.

Sandy Neck, before the endangered species restrictions. The photo was taken by Cary Wolinsky, courtesy of Massachusetts Audubon Society.

Guardians at the gate
Diamondback terrapin, photo courtesy of Robert Button; piping plover chick, photo courtesy of Steve Heaslip.

Chapter Twenty Nine

PAX VOBISCUM

Indians no longer summer on Sandy Neck. Northern right whales are endangered and close to extinction and the inshore whaling industry has faded into the mists of history. The canoes, packets, sailing ships and dories that once frequented the Harbor have disappeared. Barnstable clams, once plentiful and a source of extensive employment, are now hard to find even in small quantities. The trap fishing industry, actively pursued through the 1950s, is remembered only by those of us who have survived and known the thrill of netting giant tuna and returning home in 40 foot boats filled with tuna and mackerel. Both species have been over fished and are seldom caught today. The Eskimo curlew, once a common visitor, is extinct and seals and black-crowned night heron in and around the Harbor have been virtually exterminated. Horseshoe crabs, after 400 million years on earth, are threatened.

Throughout these pages, change is a constant.

Our religion, our culture, our recent history, our shelter, our ways of life have resulted in a worrisome disconnect with the natural world. We are told the Indians revered and acted as careful stewards of the land that provided their sustenance and home. For them thoughtless reduction of a food source could mean starvation. We have been spendthrift and prodigal with our heritage.

Some of our casual, exploitive tendencies may stem from the first chapter of Genesis.

> *"And God said, Let the waters bring forth*
> *abundantly the moving creature that hath life,*
> *and fowl that may fly above the earth in the open*
> *firmament of heaven.*
>
> *And God created great whales, and every living*
> *creature that moveth, which the waters brought forth*
> *abundantly, after their kind, and every winged fowl*
> *after his kind: and God saw that it was good.*

And God blessed them, saying, Be fruitful,
and multiply, and fill the waters in the
seas, and let fowl multiply in the earth.

...

And God said, Let the earth bring forth
the living creature after his kind, cattle,
and creeping thing, and beast of the earth
after his kind: and it was so.

And God made the beast of the earth after
his kind, and cattle after their kind, and
every thing that creepeth upon the earth
after his kind: and God saw that it was good.

And God said, Let us make man in our image,
after our likeness: and let them have dominion
over the fish of the sea, and over the fowl of the
air, and over the cattle, and over all the earth, and
over every creeping thing that creepeth upon the earth.

So God created man in his own image, in the image of
God created he him; male and female created he them.

And God blessed them, and God said unto them,
Be fruitful, and multiply, and replenish the earth,
and subdue it: and have dominion over the fish of
the sea, and over the fowl of the air, and over
every living thing that moveth upon the earth."

But what does "dominion" imply. It cannot rationally be read to justify slaughter of buffalo, right whales, Eskimo curlew or the seals in Barnstable Harbor. On the contrary, it must impose a duty of stewardship on those of us capable of protecting the creatures that cohabit the earth with us. One friend berated the geese on our golf course pointing out they were not dues-paying members: no, but as fellow inhabitants of this planet and God's creatures they do deserve, at the very least, consideration and respect. We are entrusted with the responsibility of preserving the life around us for the benefit of our children and their descendants. Whatever our religion, it must encompass concern for our one world. With swelling populations and careless exploitation, striking a better balance between humans and their environment calls for skill, caring and dedication.

Experiencing wilderness and wild creatures helps us reconsider our casual promiscuity and gives birth to the respect needed for preservation and, where required, restoration. Long strides have been taken to accomplish these goals during my lifetime. Millions of dollars have been spent and lives devoted to bringing back from the brink of extinction dwindling populations of whooping cranes and California condors. Closer to home we have extensive programs to save piping plover, least terns and other endangered species. On the Cape we have 18 or more land trusts devoted to preserving open space and there are national and international programs devoted to the same end. Bird watching has become one of the major participatory sports in the United States. Eco-tourism is a booming industry, sometimes threatening the rare species it has been designed to display: doing them in with love, so to speak. But in all of this there is hope.

Daily news on the Neck is written as footprints in the sand on a slate wiped clean by the wind. Here passed a deer and there a browsing raccoon. Shy creatures live their lives just beyond our ken and the sands bear record to scrambling mice, the wrinkled passage of a snake and to other delicate and less delicate events. Awareness of this other world seeds curiosity and interest in the creatures that share our planet. So do the dunes invite exploration and discovery. In the middens bits of pottery and the rare arrowhead may be found. Pieces of whalebone still turn up in the middle of the Neck, where great fires in days gone by consumed most of the virgin trees for boiling down whale blubber. Diligent searches produce rusted smoke bombs dropped in World War II and in the low places are the wild cranberry bogs that enticed Braley Jenkins and his young pickers to Sandy Neck The crests and troughs of the ever changing dunes afford promise of new discoveries and reawaken the wonder and curiosity of childhood. And each discovery stimulates new sensitivity and a taste for knowledge about our wild neighbors and earlier times along this wild stretch of barrier beach.

In wilderness there is solace. Walks in wild places along a beach or woodsy path, a blue sky with cotton-candy clouds, sunrises and sunsets, unspoiled natural beauty, the moon and milky way and the multiple voices of nature all are restorative. The wind-blasted pine that survives in the dry, hot sand, the multitudes of swallows that fatten up on waxy bayberries preparing for their long flight south, the fecund marsh and the tenacity of life all are age old miracles that we disrupt at our peril. And these and like miracles we must see, experience and appreciate if we are to revalue and recover the oneness with nature that invites and compels dedication to saving our wild world. In living in the wild we gain appreciation and motivation for its perpetuation.

In the wild there are no deadlines and time becomes a more congenial companion. Sunrise and sunset, the waxing and waning moon, the ebb and flow of the tides, the changing seasons are natural rhythms that dominate and set the pace of life. The cycles bring change and reinvigoration and we find ourselves no longer on an accelerating treadmill. Visiting and living in our remote marsh and dunes produces rare fellowship for all ages. The brisk water, the clean air with its salty tang and outdoor exercise promote good appetites and good humor. Companionship is at its uninterrupted best, particularly where love prevails.

May you all experience your own wild and quiet place and reap there rich rewards, and may peace be with you.

Chapter Thirty

THE CHANGING SEASONS

As the seasons change, the Little House stands as a constant in our hearts, its red chimney barely visible to the naked eye from the Barnstable shore. Early one January a young friend talked several of us into walking out to see the sunrise. We left at 5:00 A.M. in 22 degree temperature. The sky was bright with stars and with the tail wind we made destination in about an hour and a quarter. Well chilled we turned and walked back into the wind leaving the rising sun and frostbite somewhere behind. Another day after a snow several of us treked out on cross-country skis. The snow was old and high tides had flooded our trail. Worse yet, where there was snow, it was layered over with blown sand. Skiing through slush ice or on sandpaper leaves much to be desired. Most memorable our son's question "Dad, is this supposed to be fun?" One late January we had a nice walk down the back beach to the house. Crossing over we jumped a short-eared owl and watched several horned larks close at hand. Then there was the warm January night Sue and I decided to hike out and sleep over. It took time to organize and was 11:00 P.M. by starting time. It was balmy and windless and there was a bright moon. Earlier in the month there had been a great storm with extreme high tides. Later we learned about a syzygy, a lining up of the sun, moon and earth, causing higher than usual flood tides which, coupled with strong winds, can do historic damage. In any case when we arrived the door had to be forced open and high water had buckled the floor making it difficult if not unsafe to cross. By this time it was well after midnight. We were able to find an old army blanket mummy bag which we tried to curl up in on the porch. Possibly big enough for a mummy, it was much too small for mummy and daddy. So finally we decided to give in to the discomfort and fear of a plummeting thermometer and headed home. Crossing to the back beach seemed the only sensible way and that's how we walked. We got home around five and had a good morning's sleep.

February and March on Cape Cod are months to spend in a comfortable chair by your fire. Meanwhile, outdoors in March, ospreys and piping plover return to Sandy Neck to establish their breeding territories. Their return heralds a change of season.

April can bring warm days but the water is clear and cold. Soon the bass will be back. The Harbor is still alive with small flocks of black duck, eider, old squaw, sheldrake and scoters. Early one April Ned, then a college freshman, and a contemporary, paddled over to the Neck and

> ...messed around...Tipped over on the way back
> & had cold and frightening swim 100-200 yards
> ashore. Abandoned canoe which was found three
> days later floating upside down off mouth of canal
> - with one paddle in it and one floating next to it.
> I had tried searching for it up Harbor but had
> misread tides. Luckily no real loss. Ned had tried to
> stay with canoe & might have been in real trouble.

It's May and the bass are back. This is a log note from early in the month in 1979.

> Watched seven or eight seals on Great Thatch -
> one swam close to our canoe.... Woke to inane
> babble of brown thrasher.

Later in the same week we saw 10 to 20 seals at the same place but never that many since.

By late May the marsh grasses gradually begin to show green and the dead look of winter gradually melts away. The beach plums are in blossom and the hudsonia is just beginning to bloom. The Harbor is alive with many shore birds and horseshoe crabs appear, sometimes in breeding pairs, but not nearly as plentiful as formerly. Barn swallows have nested under the Little House. As the month ends the fishing gets better and better.

> We have resident willets in the grass - one nesting?
> Jeb caught a couple of bass this morning - George
> and Joe caught 22 the other morning, biggest around
> 8 lbs.... Steve Hazard says he's been fishing off the

Barnstable shore using fly rod & spinning gear - & caught more fish on flies.

When we could keep the two and three pound stripers, in May we would walk out and fish off the Indian Trail flats catching our breakfast or dinner, keeping the live fish tied to a line around our waists. Wading in shorts in the cold May water was bone chilling: nothing could make a hot shower feel better.

By early June the marsh is a lovely, soft green, water in the pot holes approaches 70 degrees, the Harbor is ready for swimming and the piping plover are nesting. One year on opening up we found a dead kestrel in the house, one that must have entered through the chimney. By the middle of the month

Roses are in bloom here and a few yellow flowers are still showing on the hudsonia....Walked to the back beach this morning. We could see 8-10 beach buggy campers. Not packed, at least like late summer.

With July and August come the best family pastimes and picnics at the Neck. Cranberries bloom in early July and the month's greenheads are a challenge. Old wives would have it that they mostly disappear with the first full moon in August but some always miss their cue. The dunes at midday become almost too hot for barefeet. The Harbor teems with bird life feeding on the new crop of bait. The water warms for comfortable swimming; racing sailboats with colorful spinnakers burst into bloom.

Nothing's better than a summer day...

and all's well with the world. Fishing in the Harbor tails off in July but August brings blue fish, if and when they choose to come. The delights reach their crescendo in August.

It's a lovely blue green day with a north wind & a touch of fall - welcome after a long spell of very hot, muggy weather. The greens of the marsh grass are dazzling...There are migrating herons and egrets here and it's only early August. The world is full of change. Only the sun, the marsh, the clouds are constants and so beautiful.

This is a mid-August note

> Sea lavender is in bloom. Beach plums are not quite ripe. Spent today waiting for the tide. Fine pastime.

By the end of the month the beach plums ripen and

> The marsh is already touched with gold, the recent full moon tides have brought cold water into the Harbor & there's a hint of fall in the air.

Then comes September with great schools of migrating bass and blues.

> The 10th. Beach plums in profusion - a banner crop after our long, hot summer with 6 inches less rain than usual - and they are big, dusty blue-purple and perfectly ripe. ...

> > Thatcher met a skunk
> > And stunk!

> The 16th. It's getting even more brilliantly September. We've seen cormorant but, surprisingly no ducks... swallows are here feeding on bayberries, getting ready to fly to points south. The road behind the house is spattered with purple bayberry seeds dropped by the birds.

> The 24th. HUGE flocks of tree swallows swarming about: but the big excitement was a kestrel in the cabin. He flew out the door and seemed fine. Cranberries galore but not quite ripe. Crickets cricketing.

> The 27th. Counted ten great egrets and seven great blue heron at low tide fishing the pools to the north of Great Thatch sharing the bounty with a couple hundred gulls, including many laughing gulls. Blue fish have been breaking for the last week or so around Phillis and even between Great Thatch and the house. We're waiting for the tide - very strenuous....

Come October and November, the blacks, eider, sheldrake and coot (the local name for scoters) are back flying in skeins overhead. In October the cranberries are ready to harvest requiring special late season trips to the Little House.

> October 4th. Got about 20 pounds of cranberries. ...We walked back through a flock of tree swallows gassing up on bayberries for their long flight somewhere....
> The grass is just golding and we've seen ducks - not big flocks.
> Terns are still here and last night, spent on the porch, ... we heard an owl asking "who...who...who".

The weather cools gradually moderated by the ocean which is slower to cool than the land. This is the time for duck hunters to refurbish their decoys, re-thatch their blinds and to time their hunts around the relentless tides. When freezing sets in, keeping a rig of decoys in place without being cleaned out by tide-driven ice, is sheer luck. The mornings and evenings are glorious and duck shooters and their dogs work the marsh. With today's restrictions, at least in Barnstable Harbor where shooting conditions are difficult, it's doubtful whether all our local hunting sets the duck population back much.

The Little House by Charles M. Harden.

In winter we see little or nothing of the Little House. Once in a while we will walk out and even spend a night. Often we walk down the back beach with binoculars to see winter birds. Once we found a dovekie high on the sand and another time a seal pup. One quiet evening late in the duck season, in the canoe, Buff, our golden retriever, and I were floating home on the last of an outgoing tide and drifted past a snowy owl perched on an ice block. A rare moment and experience to convene at dusk with such an unexpected visitor from the far north. Finally winter releases its grip and spring returns with thoughts of reopening the Little House and, if necessary, displacing the winter's raccoons or other uninvited guests.

Watching the changing seasons with the Little House in the mind's eye adds a certain cachet to life on this earth. On cold winter nights it is comforting to remember the Little House, a toasty fire in its fireplace and

The gentle chirping of millions of cricket musicians,
filling the night with their lullabies.

Race day with spectators at Beale's Pier (later the Barnstable Yacht Club). Circa 1890.

ACKNOWLEDGMENTS

This patchwork of fact and stories could never have happened without the help of many people interested in the history of Barnstable and Cape Cod. They have made the author beneficiary of frequent and generous commitments of time and prized personal notes and photographs. Without these contributions this book would have been thin indeed and to all I am thankful and indebted.

Much of the research was accomplished at the Sturgis Library in Barnstable where Lucy Loomis, Diane Nielson, Elizabeth Payne and others of its able staff directed me to the library's outstanding local and genealogical materials and reintroduced me to the rich possibilities of its records on microfische. Also they were good about obtaining books from other libraries which helped enrich the book's historical and ecological background material.

The Whelden Library in West Barnstable is a treasure trove of information about the history of that village, particularly about the Finnish people who settled there and learned to work the Great Marsh. One of the villagers, Martin Wirtanen, after retirement, became an outstanding local historian and helped to preserve related papers and photographs in the library's collection. He was a generous source of information and leads to new facts. Sadly he did not live to see and recognize his contributions to this book.

Mary Sicchio of the Nickerson Room at Cape Cod Community College has amassed a considerable folder of material concerning prohibition on the Cape. She generously shared that and her knowledge of local affairs.

Individuals who helped with anecdotes, amusing and otherwise, include Taisto Ranta, a major contributor; Duncan Oliver, one of the authors of *Cape Cod Shore Whaling America's First Whalemen*; Tim Coggeshall, a rich fund of first-hand knowledge about Barnstable pleasure sailing; Dan Knott, a long-time resident of Barnstable, boat builder and model maker without peer; Tom Marcotti, Barnstable's shellfish biologist; and Becky Harris, Director of Massachusetts Audubon's Coastal Water Bird Program, who provided data about the recent but fragile successes with breeding populations of least terns and piping plover.

No little thanks is owed to early readers, Susan Littlefield, Gerry Livingston, Tom Adams, Pete Wesselhoeft, Joe Segar and my wife, all of whom were encouraging and spared withering comments. They, in fact, worked patiently and hard over an early and crude draft and gave many thoughtful and valued suggestions.

Permission to use treasured photographs, drawings, paintings and to quote from old records has been generously provided by Robert Mesrop, whose painting of the Little House is used as cover of this book; Anne Packard, who in earlier years came to know and love Sandy Neck as few others; James Otis Ellis, who fished commercially out of Barnstable while it lasted; Charlie Harden, a local print maker, photographer and artist who continues to find inspiration in Sandy Neck as well as fish in Barnstable Harbor; Jane Layton, whose great blue heron portrait head graces Chapter Twenty Three; Peter Auger, who has dedicated much of his life to preserving Sandy Neck and teaching others to cherish it; Richard French, who found and loaned use of the early gunning notes quoted in Chapter Nine; Michael Segar, a family friend whose photographs of the Little House capture its haunting beauty; and Robert Button, a professional photographer who contributed photographs to use at no cost in the interest of protecting Sandy Neck. Technical assistance with the illustrations in the book has been provided by Michael Wardman.

Jim Coogan, a popular, well-known Cape Cod writer, was kind enough to offer encouragement and extensive help with the process of getting a book published and to the market. Donald Stewart contributed valuable marketing advice. Ben Muse examined an early proof and gave valuable suggestions about the visual qualities of the book.

The book's guiding genius in layout and make-up is the publisher, Nancy Viall Shoemaker, whose enthusiasm and technical skills have been critical in bringing the project to fruition.

BIBLIOGRAPHY

Note

The following short titles are used in the book and in the chapter notes below.

Full Reference	Short Title
The Story of the Pilgrim Fathers by Edward Arber published in 1897 by Houghton, Mifflin & Co.	*Arber's Pilgrim Writings*
The Hydrography of Barnstable Harbor, Massachusetts by John C. Ayers. From *Limnology & Oceanography 4:448-462 (1959)*	*Ayre's Hydrography*
Of Plimoth Plantation written by William Bradford covering the early years through 1646. Published in 1898 by Wright & Potter Printing Co.	*Bradford's History*
Cape Cod Shore Whaling America's First Whalemen by John Braginton-Smith and Duncan Oliver published in 2004 by The Historical Society of Old Yarmouth.	*Cape Cod Shore Whaling*
A Relation or Journal of a Plantation Settled at Ply mouth by Edward Winslow (1624) is set forth in Volume 8 of *Collections of the Massachusetts Historical Society (1801)*. The document is restated in *Arber's Pilgrim Writings* with spelling more accessible to modern readers so quotes and page references from *Arber's Pilgrim Writings* have been used rather than from the copy cited above.	*Good News from New England*
Genealogical Notes of Barnstable Families by Amos Otis. Revised by C.F. Swift and published in 1888 by F.B. & F.P. Goss.	*Genealogical Notes of Barnstable Families*
Cape Cod Its People and their History by Henry C. Kittredge. Published in 1930 by Houghton Mifflin Company.	*Kittredge's Cape Cod*
Mourt's Relation or Journal of the Plymouth Plantation (1621) edited by John Kimball Wiggin published in 1865 by Press of Geo. C. Rand & Avery. This document is restated in *Arber's Pilgrim Writings* with spelling more accessible to modern readers, so quotes and page references from *Arber's Pilgrim Writings* have been used rather than from the copy cited above.	*Mourt's Relation*

Development of a New England Salt Marsh by Alfred C. Redfield from *Ecological Monographs, 42:201-237, Spring, 1972.*	*Redfield's Development of a Salt Marsh*
Our Month on Sandy Neck by Jenny Kintzing and Susie Handy (1972). This unpublished report was written by high school seniors for Wheeler School. A copy is in the author's possession.	*The Girls' Report*
A log has been kept at the Little House since 1977. There are two unpublished volumes in the author's possession. Quotations from the log throughout the book are indented and italicized and have been edited only where necessary for continuity with the text of the book.	*The Little House Log*
The *Town Historical* Survey relating to the Little House is captioned *Form B- Building Area BVG Form No. 237.*	*The Little House Historical Survey*
The Barnstable Patriot	*The Patriot*
Barnstable Three Centuries of a Cape Cod Town by Donald G. Trayser with articles by others published in 1939 by F.B. & F. P. Goss.	*Three Centuries of a Cape Cod Town*
Unpublished journal kept in 1938 by Timothy Coggeshall and still in his possession.	*Tim's Journal*
Surveys of the buildings on Sandy Neck were prepared by the Town of Barnstable Historical Commission in the 1980s to support its request that the structures be listed on the National Register. Copies of these surveys are on file at the Commission's Hyannis office.	*Town Historical Surveys*
What We Cook on Cape Cod by Amy Handy published in 1916 by The Shawme Press, Inc.	*What We Cook on Cape Cod*

NOTES

Part One   Barnstable Harbor, The Great Marsh and Sandy Neck

The Timothy Dwight quote is from pages 49 and 50 of volume III of his *Travels in New England* edited by Barbara Miller Solomon published in 1969 by The Belnap Press of the Harvard University Press.

Chapter One   Pathway To The Sea
<u>Sources and Reading of Interest</u>
The story of John Billington is told in *Mourt's Relation pp. 112-117.* For other coverage see *Bradford's History* p. 124, *Kittredge's Cape Cod* pp. 34-35 and for the fullest detail *Mayflower* by Nathaniel Philbrick, published by Penguin Group (USA) in 2005 at pp. 110-113.

Volume I of the *Genealogical Notes of Barnstable Families* records the story of Capt. Rymer and the *George and Ann* pp. 305-310. The related quotes are from pp. 309 and 310. The circumstances of the deaths of Thomas Delap and his brother-in-law are described in the quote from page 313 of the same volume.

Facts about the tides of the Harbor are derived from *Ayers Hydrography* pp. 449-450. For further information on the subject see (i) *Redfield's Development of a Salt Marsh* pp. 205-207 and (ii) *The Tides of the Waters of New England and New York* by Alfred Redfield published in 1980 by William S. Sullwold Publishing, Inc.

Chapter Two   The Haying Fields
<u>Sources and Reading of Interest</u>
See the notes for Chapters Three and Four for more on the First Comers.

For geological history and physical facts, I have relied on *Redfield's Development of a Salt Marsh* pp.201.

For further information on the Great Marsh see Redfield's *Development of a Salt Marsh* and his *Ontology of a Salt Marsh Estuary* printed in Vol. 147 of *Science* pp. 50-55 January 1, 1965.

Books of interest on related subjects are: *Sand Dunes and Salt Marshes* by Charles Wendall Townsend published in 1913 by The Page Company; *Beach Grass* by the same author published in 1923 by Marshall Jones Company; and *Ecology of Salt Marshes and Dunes* by D.S. Ranwell published in 1972 by Chapman and Hall Ltd.

The quotes are from the cited issues of *The Patriot*.

Chapter Three   The Fantastical Beach
<u>Sources and Reading of Interest</u>
For the source of the Dwight quote, see the note above for Part One. Physical facts are from *Redfield's Development of a Salt Marsh*. The quote from *Cape Cod Shore Whaling* is from pages 29 and 30. For further information on First Comers and inshore whaling, see *Three Centuries of a Cape Cod Town* pp. 27 and 324-325, respectively.

Chapter Four   Try Yard Meadow

<u>Sources and Reading of Interest</u>

For more detail concerning the 1715 division of lands on Sandy Neck, see *Records of the Proprietors of the Common Lands in the Town of Barnstable, Massachusetts 1705-1795* edited by Andrea Leonard published in 1996 by Heritage Books.

Three Centuries of a Cape Cod Town lists the First Comers on page 27 and refers to the division of the common lands and organization of the Proprietors on page 464. The "as equal in value..." quote is from *Records of the Proprietors of the Common Lands in the Town of Barnstable, Massachusetts (1703-1791)* edited by Andrea Leonard and published by Heritage Books in 1996.

Chain of title data is derived from *The Little House Historical Survey*. The burning of the county house is described in *Three Centuries of a Cape Cod Town* pp. 360-362 with the Josiah Hinckley quote on page 362.

Mr. Hinckley's quoted obituary is from the December 4, 1883, issue of *The Patriot*.

Chapter Five   Principal Players

<u>Readings of Interest</u>

The three books by Henry Kittredge are Cape Cod literature at its best. Each is highly recommended reading for anyone interested in the Cape and its history.

Chapter Six   Sail Ho!

<u>Sources and Readings of Interest</u>

The extortionist activities of the *H. B. M.'s Spencer* and Captain Raggett during the War of 1812 are described in *Three Centuries of a Cape Cod Town* pp. 142-144. The quotation is from page 142.

Facts about the packets that plied between Cape ports and Boston are derived from chapter 17 of *Three Centuries of a Cape Cod Town* pp.251-258 and *Kittredge's Cape Cod* pp. 232- 238. Both references in the course of the cited pages tell about the race between the *Commodore Hull* and the *Mail*. The quotation from *Kittredge's Cape Cod* comes from pp. 234-235.

Quotations are from the cited issues of *The Patriot*.

People interested in ship wrecks, salvage operations and local piracy will enjoy *Mooncussers Of Cape Cod* by Henry C. Kittredge published in 1938 by Houghton Mifflin Company.

Chapter Seven   Braley Jenkins and his Cranberries

<u>Sources</u>

The quote about Deacon Braley and the one about Braley Jr.'s cranberry picking on the Neck are from Elizabeth Jenkins' article entitled *West Barnstable* included in *Three Centuries of a Cape Cod Town*. See pages 453 and 455-456, respectively. Volume I of the *Cape Cod Library of Local History* at page 87 reports Deacon Braley's long working hours and tells about his precise estimate of necessary materials for the Nantucket house. The obituary of Braley the younger is in the cited issue of *The Hyannis Patriot*, an affiliate of *The Patriot*. The report of his property sold at auction is from the cited issue of *The Patriot*.

Chapter Eight   Introducing the Little House
Sources
The quotation from the records of the Barnstable Historical Commission is from *The Little House Historical Survey*.

Chapter Nine   Gunning
Sources and Reading of Interest
The quotes from *Mourt's Relation* as restated in *Arber's Pilgrim Writings* are from pages: 408 about the store of fowl; and 436 about Plymouth Harbor. The recommendation about a desirable fowling piece is from *Good News from New England* (see *Arber's Pilgrim Writings* page 493).

The quotation from Thomas Morton's *New English Canaan* is from page 67 of the 1969 edition published by D.A. Capo Press, a division of Plenum Publishing Corporation.

The quotation from *Bradford's History* is from page 127.

The note book, comprised of only seven remaining pages, was kept by Frederick Lowell and others at their Sandy Neck camp with entries from 1896 through 1902. The note book is owned by and in the possession of Richard B. French. The quotes and data are from pages two through five.

Birds of America was edited by T. Gilbert Pearson and published in 1940 by Garden City Publishing Company, Inc. The quote is from Part I pp. 254-255.

For more about coot shooting with Shirley Lovell in Barnstable, see Chapter IV *Down Barnstable Way* from *A Book on Duck Shooting* by Van Campen Heilner published in 1939 by The Penn Publishing Company.

Chapter Ten   The Independent Project
Source
The italicized daily observations, separate reports and other quoted phrases are from *The Girls' Report*.

Chapter Twelve   The Learning Curve
Sources
Indented and italicized inserts are quotes from *The Little House Log*.

Chapter Thirteen   A Grand Clam
Sources
The Harry J. Turner, Jr. quotations are from an article entitled *Clams*, the date and source for which I have not found. His article is my source for the quote from Lt. de Broca's report to the French government.

The quote from *The Boston Cook Book* is from pages 180-181.

Frederick Atwood's unpublished narrative is dated March 7, 1974. A copy is in the possession of the Whelden Library in West Barnstable.

Chapter Thirteen   A Grand Clam (continued)

The recipe from *What We Cook on Cape Cod* comes from page 5 and the excerpt from the Lincoln poem from the foreword.

The quotation about the drowning is from the cited issue of *The Patriot*.

Mr. Dottridge's quotations are from *Reports of the Officers of the Town of Barnstable for 1927*, page 142 and for 1928, page 137. Both reports were published by F.B. & F.P. Goss.

Chapter Fifteen   Lost Innocents
Sources

The information about black-crowned night herons is primarily from the first volume of *Birds of Massachusetts and other New England States* written by Edward Howe Forbush and published in 1929 by Norton Press. The quotation is from pages 338-341. Further and current data is from *Birds of Massachusetts* by Richard R. Viet and Wayne R. Petersen, published by Massachusetts Audubon Society in 1993.

The information about bounties paid for seals are from *Town Reports* for the years in question.

Chapter Sixteen   More Gifts from the Sea
Sources and Reading of Interest

My most rewarding source for rum running data has been *Rum War at Sea* by Malcolm F. Willoughby published in 1964 by the United States Government Printing Office. Malcolm Willoughby was a Coast Guard officer and his book is the Coast Guard's official history of the era.

The Bake at Barnstable (1925) was privately published. A copy is at the Sturgis Library in Barnstable. The quote is from page 18.

Many of my facts are derived from an article by Reid Higgins dated May 1978 *Running Rum and the Roaring Twenties* included in a bound volume at the Sturgis Library titled *Historical Society of Santuit and Cotuit*.

Chapter Seventeen   Messing Around in Boats
Sources

The story of the cruise of the seven teenagers and the related quotes are from *Tim's Journal* supplemented by recent discussions with some of the participants. Tim Coggeshall provided most details concerning the development of pleasure sailing in the Harbor.

Chapter Eighteen   A Harbor Delicacy
Sources

The quote from *Mourt's Relation* is from page 408 of *Arber's Pilgrim Writings*. The quote from Thomas Morton's *New English Canaan* (1637) is from the edition published in 1969 by D.A. Capo Press, a division of Plenum Publishing Corporation.

The first edition of Fannie Farmer's *The Boston Cooking-School Cook Book* came out in 1896. The 1930 edition was published by Little, Brown and Company. *The Cookbook of "Oscar" of the Waldorf* was published by The Werner Company in 1896.

Chapter Nineteen   Other Visits

<u>Source</u>

The quotes in italics are from *The Little House Log*.

The reference to the *Speckled Band* is to the Arthur Conan Doyle story of that name found in many collections including the worn edition that came with the Little House: *Adventures of Sherlock Holmes*, published in 1892 by Harper Brothers.

Chapter Twenty   More Delicacies

<u>Sources</u>

The quotation from Thomas Morton's *New English Canaan* is from the edition cited in the notes for Chapter Eighteen above.

Facts about quahogs (today's preferred spelling) are from David Belding's *The Quahaug Fishery of Massachusetts* (1912) republished by the Commonwealth as *Marine Fisheries Series - No. 2*. Belding's definition of "treading" is on pages 32 and 33: his references to the Harbor are from page 30.

The *Bradford's History* quote is from page 157.

For the stuffed clam recipe, see page 176 of *The American Heritage Book of Fish Cookery* by Alice W. Houston published 1980 by American Heritage Publishing Co., Inc.

Chapter Twenty One   Fish Stories

<u>Sources and Reading of Interest</u>

The indented and italicized inserts are quotes from *The Little House Log*.

Anyone interested in fishing in the Harbor should read about Roccus the bass in *The Shining Tides* by Win Brooks published in 1952 by William Morrow and Company.

Chapter Twenty Three   Bird Notes

<u>Sources and Reading of Interest</u>

The indented and italicized inserts are quotes from *The Little House Log*.

The William Blake quote is from his *Songs of Innocence* (1789).

For details about Mr. Auger's thesis, see the note for Chapter Twenty Eight.

Facts about bird migration and, particularly about the ruby-throated hummingbird, are derived from *The Complete Encyclopedia of Birds and Bird Migration*, a Marshall edition published in 2003 by Chartwell Books, a division of Book Sales, Inc. For anyone interested in bird migration and the risks migrating birds incur, I recommend Brian Harrington's *The Flight of the Red Knot* published by W.W. Norton & Company in 1996. To study an entertaining obsession for birds, there's no better place to start than *King Bird Highway*, written by Kenn Kaufman and published in 1997 by Houghton Mifflin Company.

Log Book for Grace was written by Robert Cushman Murphy and published by The Macmillan Company in 1947. The quote is from page 116. The book is the log he kept for his new wife, Grace, during his two year voyage on the whaling brig *Daisy*. It was first published 35 years after his 1912 marriage and immediate embarkation on the *Daisy*.

Chapter Twenty Four   Dune Beasties

Sources

The indented and italicized inserts are quotes from *The Little House Log*.

The Robert Burns quote is from his poem *To a Mouse* from page 83 of *The Poetical Works of Robert Burns* published in 1856 by George Routledge and Sons.

Chapter Twenty Five   Sandy Neck Homesteads

Source

Information in this chapter is derived in large part from the Town Historical Surveys.

Chapter Twenty Six   Memorable Moments

Sources

The indented and italicized inserts are quotes from *The Little House Log*.

Chapter Twenty Eight   Preservation

Sources

The Peter Auger quotations are from his unpublished thesis *Sandy Neck Journal* submitted in 1973 to the Department of American Studies of Amherst College in partial fulfillment of the requirement for the degree of Bachelor of Arts with Honors. A copy of the thesis is in Mr. Auger's possession.

Chapter Twenty Nine   Pax Vobiscum

Source

The indented quote is from the *First Book of Moses*, called *Genesis* from the King James version of the *Holy Bible*.

Chapter Thirty   The Changing Seasons

Source

The indented and italicized inserts are from *The Little House Log*.

ABOUT THE AUTHOR

Descended from ancestors who came to Cape Cod in the mid 1600s, Mr. Handy's love for Barnstable Harbor and Sandy Neck is genetic. He grew up and now lives in an old family house and has sampled the delights of Barnstable for most of his 79 years. Educated at Harvard College (1951), he was a Marine officer in Korea (1952-1953), graduated from Harvard Law School in 1956 and retired from Textron Inc. in 1991 as vice president and secretary. His community service includes tours as president of the Providence Athenaeum, the Barnstable Historical Society and as a trustee of the Cahoon Museum of American Art. He is an artist member of the Providence Art Club and the Cape Cod Art Association. Ned and his wife of 57 years, Sue, have four married children and 12 grandchildren.

This book was printed on 70 lb. opaque white offset and 10 pt. Kromekote. It was designed and typeset by Nancy Viall Shoemaker of West Barnstable Press. Caslon 224 was the predominant font used - for the text and chapter heads. Caslon 224 was designed by Edward Benguiat in 1982 as an interpretation of the classic typeface Caslon (William Caslon, 1725) which was used for the printing of the Declaration of Independence. The journal entries were set in Bradley Hand, a contemporary script designed by Richard Bradley (1947-) in 1995 that shows his background in calligraphy and experimental lettering. Stone Sans (designed by Sumner Stone, a designer of type for Adobe from 1984-1989) was chosen for the captions.